THE PRAYER OF COSA

Praying in the Way
of Francis of Assisi

Cornelia Jessey

WINSTON PRESS

To Louis Vitale, OFM, and Sr. Mary Jennings, r.c.
cosa y nada

and to Molly Leddy

also, especially, to
Irving Sussman, who finds my lost things

Library of Congress Catalog Card Number: 84-51613

ISBN: 0-86683-936-4

Printed in the United States of America

5   4   3   2   1

Winston Press, Inc.
430 Oak Grove
Minneapolis, Minnesota 55403

Contents

Acknowledgments

I wish to thank Father Mark Hegener, OFM, Managing Director of Franciscan Herald Press, for the *Office of the Paters,* quotations from which are published with permission of Franciscan Herald Press, 1434 W. 51st St., Chicago, Ill. 60609.

Also, I must express my particular appreciation to Father Simon Scanlon, OFM, editor of *Way,* for his inspiration, as always.

I am grateful to all those whose work I have cited. I have chosen not to clutter the text with lengthy notes, but those works are given—in the order of their appearance—in the References section.

Introduction

When I was a child I prayed as a child. I remember praying, at the age of three or four, that my mother would find her wedding ring. It had slipped off on wash day, and she was desperately searching, turning over bundles of damp wash, shaking out sheets, curtains— the huge muddle of laundry menaced our happiness. I prayed: "God, please find Mama's ring."

The next day she found it, caught inside the fold of a net curtain, and I got the credit. Thus I embarked on prayers of petition. But as I grew up I read more about the art and craft of prayer. The eternal question, the Gospel question, was my personal question: "Lord, how shall I pray?"

I read famous teachers of prayer and was impressed with their basic rule: to empty oneself. I had to die to myself and my world and think only of God.

Naughting

The medieval teachers used the word *naughting*. Make naught of yourself, zero. I read Saint Teresa of Avila passionately, studying her mastery of the way to pray as a contemplative seeking only to experience the presence of God. Multitudes have learned from her. The Jewish philosopher-convert Edith Stein carried Teresa's word *nada* with her into the gas chamber at Auschwitz. *Nada*—the Spanish word for naughting, nothing.

When I stand off and contemplate *prayer*, it baffles me. According to anthropologists and archaeologists, prayer is something we alone of all creatures do. And we record our prayers. We seem compelled to share

prayer and to pass the words of prayer on. We raise up
monuments inscribed with our prayers. The ancient
Mayan temples are calendars of prayer. These stone
monuments were constructed with time-slots, so that
the light entering told the time of day, from dawn to
dusk, and star time, too. The light called the prayerful
to pray.

Frederick Buechner, in his spiritual memoir, *The
Sacred Journey,* writes that he sees the lives of all who
ever lived or will ever live, including his own, as "not
just journeys through time but as sacred journeys." A
sacred journey is individual and moves to a beat—not
the beat of marching feet, but the inner beat of prayer.
Contemplatives are not an elite; they are simply those
on the sacred journey who are more awake to that inner
beat. But even those of us less aware have a spiritual
potential and the same longing as we struggle for more
light on this journey.

A New Word—Cosa

The Spanish word *cosa* means "thing." It relates to the
Spanish word *nada* as the Chinese word *yang* relates to
the word *yin.* *Cosa:* thing; *nada:* no-thing; *yang:* light;
yin: dark.

Volumes have been written on the prayer of *nada,* but
nothing has been written on the prayer of *cosa,* using the
word *as a word for prayer*—because such use of the word
cosa is new. It belongs to this *fin-de-siècle,* twentieth-
century moment in our religious history. The word *cosa*
as a way of prayer is new, but the way is old: *cosa,* prayer
through things, prayer in the midst of all we are. It had
to wait for this era that has awakened to the respect
owed *things.*

Books are a sample of my things. I learned to read at
a very early age, and immediately I was lost—in the
sense that a door opened and I walked out, and it was

frustrating for my mother as she tried to get me to come back, to drag me away from whatever I was reading, which could be almost anything. Just seeing words put together in sentences—in a newspaper or magazine, on a billboard, in the Bible, in the teachings of Buddha, the *Bhagavad Gita*, the Jewish mysticism of Martin Buber, the Christian mysticism of William McNamara, the Zen ecumenism of Thomas Merton, the Russian orthodoxy of Catherine Doherty—opened the door to the world of spirituality and humanity.

At first I felt this world was my own secret garden, but soon I realized not only that it was not my own secret garden but that multitudes were there with me, and that walking amongst all of us was God, Jesus, walking on earth in the garden. And it was some garden! Not Eden nor Gethsemane but this planet Earth.

Every bit of my reading was spiritual reading, although the teachers who opened my soul to prayer were hardly canonized. They were often the despairing, such as Thomas Hardy and Fyodor Dostoyevsky and Miguel de Unamuno, Anne Sexton and John Berryman, but also the dry-eyed, compassionate recorders of our squalor, such as Charles Dickens and James T. Farrell, Graham Greene and Robert Frost and Saul Bellow.

It was in the midst of this vast medley of voices that I came upon a small green book containing both the ancient prayers of the canonical hours (the prayers of the early Church timed to the hours of the day and night) and the Canticles of Saint Francis of Assisi, also synchronized to "The Hours." It bore the title *Office of the Paters.*

Like Franny in J. D. Salinger's story *Franny and Zooey*, I came upon my teacher, my guru, in the center of *things.* Franny and Zooey, the famous sister and brother, seem to embody the search for mystical prayer,

which reached a fever point about midway in our twentieth century. In their childhood they were intellectual
American quiz kids on radio but didn't have the kind of
intellectuality called wisdom. They had instead the
intellectuality called Ph.D. or computer brains. But
they knew it, and like Oliver in Dickens's classic, *Oliver
Twist,* they asked for more. Salinger compares them to
the protagonist in Dante's *Divine Comedy,* in a forest
gone astray. They don't have a guide named Virgil, but
they do have a guide named Seymour. It is in his room,
also a secret garden with a locked door, that they find
the hidden treasure. On the back of the door, Seymour
had nailed a sheet of white beaverboard as long and
wide as the door. "Every inch of visible surface of the
board had been decorated with four somewhat gor-
geous-looking columns of quotations from a variety of
the world's literature."

Seymour had not done this as an exercise in scholar-
ship. No effort had been made to give references for
quotations, nor even to put them in categories. Salinger
describes Pascal as "unabashedly bedded-down with
Emily Dickinson," and Baudelaire's and Thomas à
Kempis's toothbrushes as hanging side by side, "so to
speak."

Entering through this door of knowledge, Franny
finds the wisdom she is seeking. There, in the midst of
the welter of *things,* she finds a small green clothbound
book (just like the one I found in the midst of my welter
of books, even green!). Hers is entitled *The Way of the
Pilgrim.*

Franny reads that all she has to do is say "Lord Jesus
Christ, have mercy on me." It is a mantra.

Having read all the books on prayer, she knows that
to attain to contemplative mysticism she must say this
mantra and synchronize it with her heartbeat—according to the teaching of the breath-prayer. She does so,
and praying the mantra with the breathing discipline

makes her faint. After she recovers she explains to her brother Zooey: "The words get synchronized with a person's heartbeats and then you're actually praying without ceasing, which has a really tremendous mystical effect on your whole outlook."

Anyone can do this, and any name of God has the same self-active power, whether it be the *Namu Amida Butsu* said over and over by one of the Nembutsu sects of Buddhism, meaning praises to Buddha, or simply the word *God* said over and over by a Christian student of contemplative prayer under the tutelage of the fourteenth-century mystical treatise, *The Cloud of Unknowing.* The word or phrase repeated and repeated to a certain beat (the heartbeat) becomes self-active, and something happens. As Franny puts it, "You get to see God."

Nada

After Salinger's book came out, everybody wanted to pray the prayer of the pilgrim. Most attractive is the idea of negating thought. You don't have to think. Just say this mantra over and over (or better still, find your own), but empty yourself of all thought and feeling and "you get to see God." Teachers came and still come from every corner of India, Asia, from anywhere and everywhere, coming out of the woodwork, so to speak, to help us find our own magic word, our own mantra.

Finally the great modern comedian of infinite despair —Woody Allen—created a scene of our freaked-out prayerfulness in his film *Annie Hall.* The scene shows a frenzied man running down a long corridor in a vast Bel Air palace, looking for a telephone. At last he finds one, dials a number, and cries, "For God's sake, help me. I forgot my mantra."

The little green book I found when I passed through the door of knowledge into the secret garden of wisdom teaches a different way of prayer. It is a way of dispersing the cloud of unknowing. The words that turn you on, turn you on to knowing. When you pray, using a word, a phrase, even a stanza, from the canticles, any of the canticles, of Francis of Assisi, the prayer becomes active, but not self-active. The canticles of Francis redirect the spiritual energies to *awareness of* things, not *away from* things. You start connecting rather than disconnecting. The poet, for Francis is a poet, presents images of this life of ours on planet Earth. The mysticism he draws you into is not abstract, and the God "you get to see" is not the transcendent God but the immediate "God who is" in the "is-ness" of our everyday life, the living God walking among us, the authentic Jesus of Christianity. So, to pray at certain hours in the mode of the Church "office," using the words of the poet Francis, is to connect with all the things of life.

Both ways of prayer have disciplines. Just as the prayer of *nada* has disciplines of posture, stillness, sitting, or the lotus position, breathing with the mantra or breath-prayer, so the prayer of *cosa* has disciplines. Just as the prayer of *nada* requires discipline of one's body, so the prayer of *cosa* requires discipline of one's time.

One night I heard Niels Bohr, the famous physicist, say on television, "The opposite of a correct statement is a false statement. But the opposite of a profound truth may well be another profound truth."

The prayer of *cosa* goes in a direction opposite to the prayer of *nada*, as north is opposite to south, but it is only another profound truth. The profound truth of the prayer of *cosa* is as old as the profound truth of the prayer of *nada*—perhaps older.

The spiritual teaching of Francis of Assisi is rooted in the Old Testament, and it flowers in Christ. Time is the structure, the hours of the day are the discipline, the Word is the touchstone to mindfulness. My body does not have to be in any particular posture; it just has to pause at certain hours and connect with God.

Time

The difference between humans and other creatures is that we humans can think of empty space, empty time. We can do what no other creature can do: We can get *out.* We can get out of time. Our ability to get out of time, to operate in a different time scale, is something we do constantly without even knowing it. We do it when we use language.

Saying one word like *emerald* or *poetry* can do it; we do it when we do arithmetic or geometry or algebra, any kind of mathematics; we do it when we sing, listen to Miles Davis's *Sketches in Spain,* play the flute, or listen to Erik Satie. We are always getting *out* of our time sequences.

And we do it when we pray. Time is the space. Right now I am doing it, getting *out* of time. Francis of Assisi tells me I can get *out,* but he also says I have to come back to this earth where I have been seeded, where I am growing up constantly to be whatever I shall be; to be present where I am, and, in the Christian mode, present to the presence of God.

To get out of time we must go into time. Time is my electric eye that opens the door.

Memory belongs to both time and eternity. I remember trying to learn to tell time when I was a small child. It was hard, and my mind rejected the whole idea that a number on the clock's face was also a space in the day.

To think too much about time can make a person feel like a stranger on this earth and in this universe. Time is not a state nor a country, yet time is a place in a space! It is the place in the space where we pray. I have to make time a place because I have to stand still in space; that takes time. It is baffling. In the early centuries the

Church didn't bother to analyze any of this, but simply
gave space names to the hours. Each hour then became
like a place wih a name. Corpus Christi! Lauds! Vespers! The name signified the hour of prayer. The
names of the hours remain, just as the place names of
places remain the same, but time itself goes on. Day
follows day, and the prayers change with each changing
day. Monday's prayers aren't the same as Sunday's
prayers, although the names of the hours are the same.

When Christian mystics pray "the divine hours," they
use time to get out of time. I like to know these things;
they are part of my species' past, and I have to know
them if I am to follow the way of contemplation with
Francis of Assisi as my teacher. I have to know about
the mystics who are my heritage and my instructors
from age to age. I have to know the mystics of the
centuries since Christ was born, walked this earth, died
and was buried and rose to immortal life, because I have
to pray in *that* context.

J. D. Salinger's novel *Franny and Zooey*, which had
such a tremendous influence on generations hungry for
prayer, seemed to send a message that all we have to do
is say a single word or phrase over and over and we "get
to see God." Somehow, few noticed that in order to
find this mantra—the Jesus Prayer—Franny and Zooey
had to go through the door of knowledge. The little
green book containing the Jesus Prayer was in the midst
of the world of words, at the center of all the great
literature our human creativity has fired up like rockets
to God.

Of course all religions use time to get out of time, but
when you go the prayer route of Francis of Assisi, you
have to use the "canonical hours" (the divine hours)
because his canticles are all in the context of Christ's
living and dying after a specified amount of time on our
planet Earth. Matins, Lauds, Prime, Tierce, Sext,

None, Vespers, Compline—these are the names of the hours.

In convents and monasteries a bell rings, and everyone stops the daily duties and makes a space for prayer. I, too, can live my week in cosmic time, where a day is as a thousand years and a thousand years as a day, and where in a single week the seven days of creation keep on happening. I don't have to go to a particular place, nor put myself in a still corner and relax and say my words, my mantra, to the breath drawn in and out. The prayer of *cosa* is not synchronized to the beat of my heart but to the beat of solar time.

An example of the prayer of *cosa* discipline is vividly presented in the musical comedy *Fiddler on the Roof.* The story on which the opera is based comes from a book, *The World of Sholom Aleichem*, by Maurice Samuel, a collection of stories about Jewish life in the Russian Jewish Pale. One of the stories tells of Tevyeh, an impoverished peddler, going home through the woods with an empty wagon. All day he has been loading and unloading logs. The ruble a day he earns will not buy food for his family of ten, including his dispirited horse. Then he realizes the sun is setting; against the weight of despair he has to lift up his heart to God.

> "But in spite of everything, we are still Jews. When evening comes we have to say our prayers. You can imagine what the prayers sounded like if I tell you that just as I was about to begin *Shmin-esra* my horse suddenly broke away as if possessed by the devil and ran wildly off through the woods. Have you ever tried standing on one spot facing east while a horse is pulling you where *it* wanted to go? I had no choice but to run after him, holding onto the reins and chanting at the top of my voice, as if I were a cantor in a synagogue: *'Thou sustainest the living with much loving-kindness* (and sometimes with

a little food) *and keepest thy faith with them that sleep in the dust . . . .* (Oh, heavenly Father, why does this happen to me? Am I not as good as others? Help me, dear God!) *Look upon our afflictions . . . .'"*

Tevyeh prays in his own way. He says the prescribed prayers, which he knows by heart, "but while his tongue follows the ritual, his mind accompanies it with interpolations and interpretations and commentaries" that are like a gathering into the net of prayer, all of his life.

A Showing

The pages that follow are not intended as a step-by-step classical prayer guide but as a showing-how, an enactment of how to pray the prayer of *cosa*. Here I am, Lord. I come to do your will. Here I am with all my needs, my world, my hard work, my tiredness, my empty wagon, my runaway horse, lifting my thoughts, my moods, my emotions to God, even while running in the wrong direction trying to hold on to my runaway horse.

Each day I begin a new day with praises, lauds, whether I feel in a praising mood or not. My jumping-off place, my diving board, is the canonical hour linked to a canticle of Francis of Assisi, because essentially I am not trying to jump off the earth but trying to take it with me—without letting go of my peddler's pack, carrying it all.

My prayer? I want to make an arc, a spark that connects with God, so for this moment I am in that arc light between heaven and earth. The week's schema that follows does not mean you do it in a week, but one week shows how it will go for all the weeks of your life. The things you gather up into your prayer—as I gather them up into mine—may be anything you've ever read or heard, fragments of other people's thoughts that caught you, fragments of the scriptures or poems, the words of a song.

Sunday Morning at Lauds

Sunday morning at Lauds, Francis of Assisi sings praises to the Sun:

> Most high, mighty and good Lord,
> Yours is the praise, the glory, the honor, and all
>   benediction.
> To you alone, Most High, do they belong,
> And no one is fit even to mention your name.
>
> *(Canticle of the Creatures)*

My first realization on this way of prayer is that the mystical poet is not praising the sun but the one who made the sun; most high, mighty and good Lord, *yours* is the praise, and no human being can grasp the meaning of your Name. Francis is a scriptural man; his canticle is rooted and grounded in the praising universe of the Old Testament, where light is the gift of gifts, and it is a made thing: God made the sun that radiates light on our planet Earth.

Francis begins with *me*—I am the human being who cannot grasp the meaning of God's name. Like the sun, I am a thing, a body, a dense yet light-reflecting body, waiting to be lit up by the sun so that I can reflect. The light that comes from beyond me is what generates my prayer. The light is my life, it is to me what the sun is to earth: *It* makes me come alive.

At dawn when I rise to praise with Francis, I praise the Lord who makes the sun. He won't let me down. The sun will rise, my earth will live, a new day will begin. Thus Sunday begins on this note: My life of prayer starts with the sun rising on the last morning of the old week and the first morning of the new week.

I wake before it is light. In his *Hagia Sophia*, Thomas
Merton reflects on the same idea as Francis, that the sun
is like the Son. As the sun penetrates the darkness all
over the world, so the Son penetrates the darkness of all
the separate beings everywhere, comes into us all, dispersing the darkness.

Here I am, trying to wake myself up while everyone is
asleep. To think of all the sleeping creatures is touch-
ing: Humans are fragile, vulnerable, when asleep. It is
confusing and frightening to think that even the killers,
the brutalized, the torturers, the death squads, the sad-
ist pornographers, the child abusers, the drug dealers,
the tyrants and dictators are all vulnerable and even
pathetic when asleep. I think of the four women missionaries tortured, raped, murdered in El Salvador, on
their way to their mission. As soon as we humans wake
up, a change of character takes place, the me turns into
a threatening ego who must destroy—rising up not to
praise the sun, but to demand a place in the sun, and if
that means taking away another's place in the sun, that
only whets the appetite.

Lord, you made the sun; yours is the praise, the glory,
the honor, and all benediction. Lord, you made the fire
that brings life to planet Earth, and death also.

It was because they recognized the savage hunger of
the ego that the great wisdom teachers such as Teresa of
Avila, John of the Cross, Buddha, and others insisted
that the ego must be annihilated. To love God I must
get my self out of the way. My *I* is blocking the view.

This Sunday morning at Lauds, taking the way of *cosa*
leads me on a different route. Instead of the self praying to be emptied, annihilated, made nothing, the self is
to be filled. All the *things* my ego-self encounters this
day on earth come with me. I want to learn to pray with

this teacher Francis of Assisi because I believe planet Earth is significant and we are blessed with all that is, or not at all.

Rise up then, woman, get out of bed, for the sun is making waves on the shore of night. Don't make waves! The Roman emperor Trajan hated the early Christians and savagely repressed them, giving as the reason that "they gather before dawn to sing a hymn to Christ as God." Maybe he hated to get up early. Some people who look gentle and harmless asleep turn into dangerous animals on awakening. Or perhaps he feared light, feared sunlight, felt threatened by a religion that praised the light, instead of cringing in the dark before the pagan gods of thunder and lightning.

Danger! Light!

When I began to study this way of prayer with Francis of Assisi, I lived in the desert and knew well the threat, the danger, of sunlight. But I also knew the dazzling clarity that came into the darkness and banished it, exposing the wonders (and horrors) of this earth.

Every morning just before dawn, my dog—an Afghan hound—leaped on the bed and stood on me. He had a clock inside his head and never needed to be told the time. He "rang the bell" for Lauds. We would go forth, I holding the leash in one hand, my little green book in the other. The dog, leaping and bounding; me, strenuously hanging onto the leash with my strong right hand, while in my weak left hand I clung to the little green book open to the prayers for that day. Today it is September, fresh after August rain.

The first rays slide over the eroded hills; they turn red. My book opens to Friday at dawn, and even though this is Sunday I read Friday's words:

AT MATINS

1. Clap your hands, all you nations, shout to God
   with a voice of rejoicing, for the Lord on high is
   terrible, the great king over all the earth. . . .
2. For our most holy Father in Heaven, our King,
   ages ago sent his beloved Son down from on
   high; and he has wrought salvation in the midst
   of the earth. . . .
3. Let the heavens rejoice and the earth exult, let
   the sea be roused and the many things filling it,
   let the fields be glad with everything in them.
   Sing a new hymn to him. All the earth, sing to
   the Lord. . . .
4. Bring to the Lord, O you countries of the Gen-
   tiles, bring to the Lord glory and honor, bring
   the Lord glory for his name. . . .
5. Bring your own person to carry his holy cross,
   and to follow his most holy commandments to
   the very end. Let all the earth be roused at his
   sight. Proclaim among the nations that the Lord
   is ruling.

The book tells me, in parentheses, that these praises
set forth here at Matins are from the "Vespers Office of
the Passions."

Clap your hands! Applause, applause! Suddenly I
realize why Francis is praising. I can hear applause for
the light. It is flowing through all the canyons, flowing
over the desert, and for Francis *that* is praiseworthy.
Light! Light is responsible for all our aliveness, so let
me applaud you, Brother Sun, you who show me everything alive right now where I am, walking over the
desert. You are physical, you are a thing, you are the
physical evidence of spirit. Clap your hands, everybody,
for ages ago God sent the Son who is like the sun, only
more so! In the midst of the dying earth, he cried out:
Life is forever. Ages ago he sent his son into the midst

of this earth to save us from nothingness. We are here for *some thing*! Let the earth exult.

A mockingbird begins to sing a complicated, ringing song. I must find this bird; where are you, bird? Now I see the feathered little ego high on the tip of a silver rod, the TV aerial on a house, singing with the total intensity of a real live bird. It levitates up, up, three or four feet into the air. That's how it sings, lifted up on ecstatic notes.

Words from a poem by William Blake enter my mind: "How do you know that every bird that cuts the airy way is an immense world of delight closed by our senses five?" Am I quoting it right? It has just come, and I know it is from Blake and remember his joy in the bird whose immense world of delight is "closed by our senses five"! He was another poet like Francis who celebrated the creation of *things*.

The dog cannot bear another moment of standing still contemplating the wonderful exaltation of the mockingbird carried up into pure space. The dog has his own intensities of excitement, responding to the beams of sunlight. He, too, must move. He leaps, races, and can hardly stand still long enough to smell every bush and lift his leg. He must keep moving, and he keeps me moving. Everything is moving, for the sun brings a stir in the air. Francis sings the praises of all that moves:

> Be praised, my Lord, for all your creatures,
> In the first place for blessed Brother Sun,
> Who gives us the day and enlightens us through
>   you,
> Beautiful and Radiant, giving witness of you,
>   Most High.

The words are from his *Canticle of the Sun.* It has been translated by different translators, and I have copied

many different versions into my book, but whose is
whose? Who knows? They are part of me now, my own.

We are here to witness, but not passively. Contemplation means to witness and to respond. The light breaks
into my darkness, the sunlight speaks to me, reminds me
that I am me. It wakes up my mind as well as my body,
and thoughts like silver grunion come up through the
sea of my consciousness and subconsciousness to strew
the shores. I can catch some of the little fish and eat
them; the rest will die. But those I catch and eat fill me
with nourishment. All the books I read, the people who
have come into my thoughts, the work I do, the animals
that are part of my life, the shouts of children, computer
games, even bingo—all these things and much much
more are parables of spirit. My earth is a fleshly and a
mystical creation.

Be praised, my Lord, for all your creatures—in the
first place for blessed Brother Sun. This meditation
makes me stand still at times and ponder the way Francis
thought of the sun. He did not praise the sun as Ra, nor
as the ancient Mayan tribes and other mystics have
praised the sun, as their god, bowing to it, worshipping
it. Francis praised Brother Sun as a creature, as much a
creation as all creatures are, so he praised God for making this creature, Brother Sun. He praised *the making*
because he was in love with the *maker* of all making.

The dawn light evokes things sharply visible on the
desert; I see new dimensions, folds in the hills that I
never saw before, clefts and peaks. Francis walked in
parables of sunlight; he saw the world filled with the
presence of Christ and thought God's descent into flesh
was a terrible grandeur.

The dog puts his nose into a burro bush, and for long
moments we stand still while he sniffs out the very soul
of the burro bush with his flat camel's nose—seeking a
symbolic woodchuck there in the depths of the earth.

We are just standing. I look at the way the light ripples over the sandy world all around me; light glances off every grain of sand. Infinitely small, hitherto unseen, unnoticed, white flowers open before my eyes. Small insects are moving over this land, carrying large boulders. Tiny butterflies, yellow and white, rise up out of the flowers—"Why, they do nothing but leap for joy in their mother's womb, like little John the Baptist."

It is another fragment of poetry that floats up out of my soul, or subconscious, or wherever the things I read are stored—I know it is from the poet Rilke, who loved to walk out at dawn and see all the tiny insects springing up out of hidden seeds. The aliveness of everything as the light vibrates through the atmosphere and reveals the realities of my real world is like an electrical current that charges all the connections. I see everything in a different light (to coin a pun). My world lights up, a great constellation that includes all things, trees and birds, sticks and stones, things of the imagination, fragments of poetry, phrases from the Psalms, scriptural readings, songs, scenes from operas, pieces of sculpture, a stone hand, computer chips, TV shows, robots, a mouse, streets, houses, trails etched on the sand by sidewinders, paintings of squares and triangles and of horses; Coltrane and the jazz improvisations; a couple of chuckawalla lizards dancing together on top of this greenly resinous creosote bush; the burgeoning brown crickets after the rain.

Earth

I love this earth and all it contains; I love the fish in the sea, the beasts on the land, the birds in the air, the dark reaches of outer space with strangely illuminated planets and constellations, which swing within my range of vision. I witness from millions of light years away their terrifying theatre and applaud from my safe distance. I do not want it to be that God is *real* but the earth is an *illusion* and I myself am an illusion even more illusory than earth. The mystical love I seek to contemplate includes all that *is*—and all that is not, in the sense of things I have not seen, have no experience of except through projections of my imagination—in the reality of God, in a spirituality of togetherness without the loss of a single thing's singularity.

As the dog and I race down a dry wash, four or five notes rise up on a tender questioning phrase—the notes of the quail. Repeated and repeated with few variations, these notes never pall. Each time I hear this simple, sweet, unanswerable question, I think the notes must be pure music like the music of the spheres.

To my mind comes Juan de la Cruz, the memory of his words about earth and its creatures—Saint John of the Cross, teacher and friend of Saint Teresa of Avila. All through the centuries Saint John of the Cross has been the mystic par excellence, the supreme Christian guru to teach all those who seek the presence of God how to ascend Mount Carmel.

> All the beauty of creatures compared with the Infinite Beauty of God is supreme ugliness. So a person attached to the beauty of any creature is extremely ugly in God's sight. A soul so unsightly is incapable of transformation into the beauty which is God, because ugliness does not attain to beauty. All the grace and elegance of creatures compared with God's grace is utter coarseness and crudity. That is why a person captivated by this grace and elegance of creatures becomes quite coarse and crude in God's sight. Accordingly, he is incapable of the infinite grace and beauty of God because of the extreme difference between the coarse and the infinitely elegant. Now all the goodness of the creatures in the world compared with

the infinite goodness of God can be called evil,
since nothing is good save God only (Lk. 18:19). A
man, then, who sets his heart on the good things of
the world becomes extremely evil in the sight of
God. Since evil does not comprehend goodness,
this person will be incapable of union with God,
who is supreme goodness.

(*The Collected Works of St. John of the Cross*)

This paragraph sums up the teaching of most of the
great teachers of contemplative prayer, today as in
times past—whether Christian or Buddhist, Zen or Sufi.

But there were always some religious geniuses who
taught a different way to experience the love and the
presence of God. Two of the greatest were Saint Bernard of Clairvaux and Saint Francis of Assisi. Thomas
Merton, who had at first thought to enter a Franciscan
religious order, recognized the connection, and wrote
of Saint Bernard of Clairvaux (in *The Last of the Fathers*):

Saint Bernard seems to have struck an altogether
new note of hope in Medieval spirituality, and it is
no exaggeration to attribute to him the current of
sweetness and joy that was to become in Francis of
Assisi a "stream of the river making the City of
God joyful" (Ps. 45:5).

Like many others, I have been deeply affected by the
vigorous spirituality of the contemporary Trappist
monk Father Merton. He, too, strikes an altogether
new note of hope for twentieth-century people, and I
think it is no exaggeration to attribute his praising and
joyfully vital prayerlife to the fact that he was taught to
swim in the "current of sweetness and joy" by those
superlative swimming instructors, Francis of Assisi and
Bernard of Clairvaux.

The teachers of self-naughting hold the center stage,
however, and have held it in all times. In our century

this teaching has been strongly reinforced by the influx of Eastern mysticism. It was as if the powerful force of nothingness as the spiritual goal, taught by John of the Cross, had met the powerful force of nothingness taught by Buddha, and these two tides on the sea of God, one coming from the west, the other from the east, had risen up in an enormous wave. The spiritual surfer was exhilarated riding that high surf, but when the seeker dropped down into the trough of nothingness, the moment of truth was nihilistic. Everything, including the earth, disappeared, like a mud ball drowned in the tidal wave.

One night I heard Peggy Lee, singer of popular ballads, sing a song, asking, Is that all there is to this life?

I don't know the song, and I only remember that sentence, but it made me think how common is this experience of our existence as a great exhilarating high of self-forgetfulness—and then? *Nada?* In The Ninth Elegy of his *Duino Elegies,* Rainer Maria Rilke expresses the same thought:

But this
having been once, though only once,
having been once on earth—can it ever be
    cancelled?

Today we are aroused to a truth we never knew before—that it all *could* be "cancelled." And for the first time we see the wonder of creation, of all made things, in a different light.

Saint Francis of Assisi has been overexposed as peacemaker and bird lover, underexposed as mystic and teacher of contemplative prayer. His theme was joyful because he really believed in *salvation,* but his idea of salvation was not like that of the fundamentalists.

Consider the word *salvation.* I am considering it and pondering how different the meaning is to me now. Not very long ago it rang with a pietistic note of doomsday, of sinners going to hell unless they were "saved." But who were the saved? Who were the unsaved? Everybody has a different answer, and ultimately only confusion and self-diminishment are the upshot.

John of the Cross stated the negative truth: Never put God's works, his creations, ahead of God. Francis of Assisi states the positive truth: To praise the grace and elegance of all creatures, including Brother Sun and Sister Moon, is not to diminish God. God is not in an adversary position to his creatures. Francis does not see the "good things of the world" as "compared with the Infinite Beauty of God"—because all that God has made is good and is the signal of his beauty. All created things are clues to the beauty of God, which eye cannot see until the work of our own personal life is completed on this earth. All this making from nothing, this *something*, is my work too, the work I am doing in and on myself!

Prayer is the great longing in the hearts of people from generation to generation, no matter whether born to a religious faith or to none. But the persistent question is echoed and reechoed: What's it all about, man? What's it all about, woman? Francis of Assisi saw this longing, this hunger, and recognized it as the hunger of those who are empty, so he taught fullness.

People were empty in his time, as I am empty in my time. I don't see how teaching me to empty myself (teaching me that thought, any thinking, destroys prayer) is going to do me much good, since I'm already an empty husk who thinks as little as possible anyway.

God wants to fill me so that I can have something to praise and feel joyful about.

Pierre Teilhard de Chardin, deeply influenced by Francis of Assisi, wrote his mystical experiences as one who had gone toward God through the prayer of *cosa*.

Not that he used the word *cosa*, but what he wrote is covered by the word:

> God, in all that is most living and incarnate in Him, is not withdrawn from us beyond the tangible sphere; He is waiting for us at every moment in our action, in our work of the moment. He is in some sort at the tip of my pen, my spade, my brush, my needle—of my heart and of my thought.
>
> (*The Divine Milieu*)

See

William Blake saw the world in a grain of sand and heaven in a wildflower, and through that seeing he held "Infinity" in the palm of his hand and "Eternity in an hour."

When Francis sings canticles of praise for our sister mother earth, for the air, for cloudy, fair, and every kind of weather, for fire and water, for the sun, for all creatures—he isn't praising ecology, nor sentimentally taking pleasure in the prettiness of birds, deer, or even the grim charm of brother wolf. He is making a mystical statement about the prayer of Light that brings us to contemplation. No saint except Thérèse of Lisieux has been written about with more banality and shallowness than Francis of Assisi.

A recent book on Saint Francis quotes one of his many biographers (not by name), who commented:

> It was the peculiar religious genius of Saint Francis that he could combine an utter seriousness with the following of Christ and a healthy love of the world, as a gift from God.
>
> (Cunningham and Stock, *Saint Francis of Assisi*)

But the unnamed writer missed the point, as many writers on Francis do. For Francis of Assisi, the love of Christ is not *in conjunction* with matter. Francis is a teacher who reveals that I must love Christ not just in the charms of nature, nor for the high I get from seeing inspiring natural beauty. I must love Christ *in matter*, even and most of all in destroyed matter, in what is sick, distorted, hurting, leprous, ugly; I must love Christ in the dying. My teacher teaches compassion. His theme is "courtesy"; in that way Francis is like the Zen masters, for their teachings, too, are "courtesy"—to render unto each thing *attention*. Render respect and helpfulness without expecting any return or response from Brother Fire except that fire will burn.

And now, at Matins, in the darkness before Lauds, in monasteries religious men and women rise while the night is at its lowest physical ebb, that darkest night before dawn, and praise God. They clap their hands, and so do I. I clap my hands and in my heart say the words that are now my own; I'm not reading them, but they are part of me: Clap your hands, all you nations, shout to God with a voice of rejoicing, for the Lord on high is terrible, the great king over all the earth.

The Lord on high is terrible in his will to save all things, including us, from our will to destroy. Francis was given a mystical insight into the whole order of creation: to see it not as a playground nor as causing an aesthete's downfall into sensual love of beauty, but as a manifestation of God. *Love* appeared to him as God's constant bringing into life, even out of death bringing life, so that all of nature, the whole universe, is to be saved. That is the way I am being taught to *see*. "Jesus, make me immortal with a kiss!"

Francis kisses the earth. The mysticism of Francis is beginning to be understood today in depth. His insight eight centuries ago had to wait for its full impact to be comprehended. Now the nuclear age is upon us. In the stark deathlight—the Hiroshima light that brings oblivion, total darkness—we are dramatically aware of the wonder of creation. The way of *cosa* is just arriving as a way of spirituality that demands of our ego a work of care, of nurturing the makings of God. God gave the human species dominion, says Scripture—but as a trust.

The way of *nada* seeks the same ideal through the negation of self, by putting ourselves and our greed *down*. But this also leads to putting everything down, for if *we* are nothing, everything is nothing. All is illusion. Merton quotes Suzuki, in *Zen and the Birds of Appetite*:

> As Buddhists would say, the realization of Emptiness is no more, no less than seeing into the nonexistence of a thingish ego-substance. This is the greatest stumbling block in our spiritual discipline, which, in actuality, consists not in getting rid of the self but in realizing the fact that there is no such existence from the first.
>
> (A dialogue by Daisetz T. Suzuki
> and Thomas Merton)

Thingishness

With a jerk that nearly knocks me off balance, I am yanked back to this place where morning is coming over the desert. The Afghan has leaped backwards as only Afghans can do, pulling me backwards. I am alerted all at once, because I've lived long enough in desert country to know the immediacy of vigilance. I look and see an ugly death struggle, lit up as the sunrays penetrate a dense thornbush. A large diamondback rattler and two young snakes are being set upon by a horde of brown crickets. The rattler turns its head from side to side, its tongue flashing in and out. It tries to coil and buzz its rattle, strikes, coils again and again, but on the third attempt to coil and strike the attackers, it fails. The crickets have weighted it down so it can barely lunge forward; the young snakes, perhaps newborn, are totally consumed while I watch. Ten or twenty minutes pass, and by the time it is all over, the large diamond-back and the young snakes are literally and utterly stripped of flesh. The brown horde moves on; crickets from the rear pause briefly over the skeletons of the snakes. Even the rattles are consumed.

We turn back. I look up. Vast reaches of space, intense clarity, pure light radiating all around this scene. Yet there are brutality and death in my garden. The light must show this also to me, and somehow I must lift it all up with Francis into my space-time, here and now at this hour of Lauds, praising! I can't forget it; I can't forget that this world of mine is a broken world.

"We must not dare ever come into God's presence alone," writes the Carmelite mystic William McNamara, in his book *Earthy Mysticism.* "God will say, 'Where are the others? Where is my broken world?' "

Here, Lord, all of it—me and my earth.

Monday Morning at Lauds

Almighty, most high, holy and sovereign God, holy and just Father, Master of heaven and earth, for your own sake we give you thanks—by your will and through your only Son, and in the Holy Ghost you have created all things spiritual and bodily.

Thus Francis sings on Sunday, but on Monday when he calls me to get up before dawn, he teaches me a working-day prayer, in the Canticle for Matins that precedes this day's Lauds. On Monday in the predawn darkness, Francis is singing to God:

You are all the wealth one can desire. You are beauty. You are gentleness. You are our protector.

This is a hard saying, teacher. The next verse, the verse for Lauds, then begins:

Be praised, my Lord, for all your creatures,
In special for his worship Brother Sun,
Who brings the day and you give light to us
    through him. . . .
He brings us understanding of you, Most High.

Well, he'd better enlighten my understanding, because right now, waking up on Monday morning, I'm being instructed by Francis at Matins that the Lord is all the wealth I can desire! At this moment I must think about this instruction given at Matins; later, maybe I'll smile at Francis's humor, calling Brother Sun "his worship." But first this matter of wealth.

"Are you joking, Lord?" At this very moment, while I'm saying "You are all the wealth one can desire," I'm getting ready for work so that I can make some money. I need it. I must have work. I also desire money. Instead of praising the Lord with "You are all the wealth I can desire," I cry out in my need, "Help me find a job today, Lord!"

Outside, the night seems darker than it was even a minute ago. The stars have gone down, and there is no ray of light except from the distant highway lamps. Will the sun rise once more this morning? Brother sun, your worship, bring the day. It's ironic that on Monday morning, in the canticle for the hour of darkness before the dawn, when I am at my lowest ebb, I am called to wake up and sing with Francis, "You are all the wealth one can desire!"

Needs

Lord, help me find a job today. I need money, I have to pay the rent, I have to buy food, I need tires, I need to get my teeth fixed, I need to get the TV repaired. You are all the wealth I can desire?

I contemplate the paradox of God's being all the wealth I can desire and yet my need to pay the rent and the doctor bills, to buy food, to get new eyeglasses: so this is what I am bringing to Lauds on Monday morning. Whilst taking this way of prayer, trying to be a contemplative so that I can experience the presence of God, I am contemplating my needs.

We all live with needs; needs are our lives. The young woman who lives across the street found out on her thirty-second birthday that she has terminal cancer. She needs a cure. Why don't they find a cure for cancer? And for AIDS? And a cure for loss of memory? The Spanish poet Rafael Alberti spent a life in exile after the Spanish Civil War in the thirties, and when he grew old he wrote sad poems and said he forgot things. Loss of memory means "your head becomes filled with blank spaces." Maybe he had Alzheimer's disease. And how about a cure for multiple sclerosis while they're at it?

I think of my needs and of the needs of my people who are the whole human species, and of my brother and sister animals, dying in the droughts of Africa, along with all the human beings dying there and everywhere.

Francis calls me to join him in a new song to God, telling God he is all the wealth one can desire, just when I am getting ready to go out and try to make some money, which I also desire. I am telling God he is all the wealth I can desire; but what is God telling me? If I turn what Francis of Assisi is singing in my ear to the other side of the recording, it could be that God is saying the same thing to me: "You, my friend, are all the wealth *I* desire!" All of *me*?

Getting it all together is what I have to do, right now —without understanding how this can be done. Scripture says you cannot serve God and mammon—the latest translation of mammon is *money*. That tells our predicament. Francis of Assisi does not say shape up; he only calls me this morning to speak the words, and in doing that I am contemplating God, as I am, with all my needs.

What is contemplation? What is mysticism? When I read about mysticism or hear lecturers on mysticism, I am told first off that mysticism is a doing: making a space. I have to make a space where I am no longer in charge of my own self, yet at the same time I am still my own self in charge! Making a space—a space for prayer, to push everything outside the space, yet bring everything inside the space?

But perhaps to make a space is *not* like sweeping everything aside. Perhaps it *is* like stepping into a different dimension, stepping out of my place into a timeless dimension. Now I can bring everything with me into that timeless dimension: *cosa*, the things so alive on this earth, all that God continually makes even as we continually destroy; but also what we make, *our* things too— our pictures on cave walls, our Rosetta stone; our things are of value. Bread, too.

Antonia White, the English novelist, says that Christianity is based on desire and that Christ comes in response to our desire; he is born in a manger in Bethlehem, which means *the house of Bread.*

Mysticism is another dimension, a space into which I can move. But the Zen teachers describe it as a *void.* "The Zen intuition of Hiu Neng is an intuition of the metaphysical ground of all being and knowledge as void," wrote Merton in *Zen and the Birds of Appetite.* To expel our dread of the void, he went on to explain that "the pure void is also pure light" and that pure light is "pure being."

The mystics are wonderfully interconnected, and I can step into this dimension and bring their thoughts with me. At this moment as I stand here, in this space— taking the space out of the time named Lauds—the thoughts of the mystics go in and out of my space. One of the thoughts that enters is something written about thought by D. H. Lawrence. I don't have the reference for it. I only copied down his words because they were good words about *thought.*

> Thought, I love thought. Not the joggling and twisting of already existent ideas. I despise that self-important game. Thought is the welling up of unknown life into consciousness. . . . Thought is a man in his wholeness wholly attending.

As for me, getting up this Monday at dawn to praise the coming of Light into my darkness, I love thought too.   That should be qualified because there are thoughts I don't love. I love the thoughts that enter my space with bright, glancing insights. But troublesome thoughts also enter—thoughts, for instance, of MX missiles, threatening to destroy everything with hate, violence,   anger,   jealousy,   competition,   rejection. Destructive thoughts.   The terrible power of the destructive thoughts that are sent forth all over the earth from those who become leaders of state! How pathetic our species is in its political existence—and what political needs we have! Hunger, world hunger, economics and hunger—they are inextricably interwoven; governments decide when solvency demands that food   production   be   limited   and   unemployment increased.

Thought is a man in his wholeness wholly attending; thought is a woman in her wholeness wholly attending. What a wonder my mind is! That is, the human mind is a wonder when enlightened, but not the banal, tedious mind that can only brood over grievances or plot evil.

The sky is becoming a morning sky, and down the street rides an old man on a bicycle, pedaling slowly, for he has a retinue. Suspended from the handlebar on the right is a rope, at the end of which a small brown terrier trots.   Suspended from the left handlebar is another rope, at the end of which a small grinning boy trots. The old man pedals along meditatively, and the two followers meditatively follow after. There is no other traffic on the road—it is too early.

Before me suddenly appears the memory, a living image out of the past, of my mother and her walker and the Afghan dog. Both grown old, she and the dog walked side by side, she with her walker and he serenely at her side. I see her old hands on the walker, thin, pale, transparent, almost childlike, so different from the strong, tan work-worn hands of her vigorous young years. She would give the walker a pat when the journey was completed without mishap, as if to say, "Well done, good and faithful servant."

In her old age she thanked God, praised him for all the practical down-to-earth helps invented for old people: the cataract eyeglasses that made it possible for her to see, and the walker that made it possible for her to get to the bathroom under her own power and to take a meditation walk around the yard with the old dog. He too, grown old, nearly blind and sadly stiff-legged with spinal arthritis, still retained some of the poetic fire of his young years, lifting his head on his long neck, still proud.

"You and me, we know." She'd give the dog a pat, risking removing one hand from her walker.

When I step out of time into space, everything can come into this dimension of spirituality. The way of *cosa* does not ask me to detach myself from memory. It is in this context the philosopher Jacques Maritain defines the essence of Christian existentialism:

> It is something to know that God is a transcendent and sovereign Self; but it is something else again to enter oneself and with all one's baggage—one's own existence and flesh and blood into the vital relationship in which created subjectivity is brought face to face with this transcendent subjectivity and, trembling and loving, looks to it for salvation.
>
> (*Existence and the Existent*)

The way Maritain thought of religion is the way I think of it: "as a relation of person to person with all the risk, the mystery, the dread, the confidence, the delight, and the torment that lie in such a relationship."

Each of us who takes this path of prayer has to bring a whole life, a life that starts far back, that includes all the people of one's life, all the animals, all the "baggage." It is often said that one of the signs of a spiritual renewal that is really *spiritual* is that everything in us is affected. Everything I read or watch on television or in the movies is affected, speaks to me differently—even pornography and crassness. I think about them in a different way, not necessarily in the context of sin, but more in the pattern of a life that is being woven in the dark.

Thomas Merton broke down the often-stupid restrictions on reading, especially on what religious people call "spiritual reading." He assigned his novices writers of novels such as Faulkner and Camus, poets and ballad singers such as Dylan Thomas and Bob Dylan.

Standing here at this hour, I think of the monks and nuns who get up in the middle of the night to pray. When Thomas Merton wrote about his first taste of this way of using time to enter into timeless space, he said:

> You lie down in your dormitory cell and listen to first one monk and then another monk begin to snore, without, however, going to sleep yourself. Then you count the quarter hours by the tower clock and console yourself with an exact knowledge of the amount of sleep you are missing. The fun does not really begin until you get up at 2 A.M. and try to keep awake in choir.
>
> (*The Sign of Jonas*)

Somehow, changing the time does amazing things to you. Merton was filled with spiritual intensity, an élan you do not get when you have gone to bed at a routine time and gotten a full eight to ten hours sleep. He found that his prayerlife was keyed up as a violin string is tightened:

Love sails me around the house, I walk two steps on the ground and four steps in the air. It is love. It is consolation. I love God. Love carries me around. I don't want to do anything but love.

(*The Sign of Jonas*)

He broke the rules of spiritual "perfection" because spiritual teachers were always warning the contemplative not to derive pleasure from prayer, no "highs," which were given the name "consolations." And how I delight in Merton's defiance of all those great teachers of nothingness, with his exalted cry: "I don't care if it is consolation!"

Puritanical bluenoses I call those teachers of a spirituality that threatens your chances for a love relationship with God if you dare show any emotional pleasure in that love. "No consolations" is supposedly the test of an authentic vocation to prayer. But what are consolations? Joy? Love? Hope? We humans are emotional beings, and the emotions must be part of all I am bringing to God, just as much as the mind that has been given me.

Consolations are what help me get out of bed at this dark hour on this Monday morning, just to get out of bed and go look for work, or stay home and take care of an old, sick parent. At such low-ebb hours I understand more clearly why Francis calls me to get up and say some words of poetry. Just to say *good* words, not magic words, just to say, "Be praised, my Lord, you are all the wealth I can desire!" There is a power in those words. They are not magic, yet my burden is eased and I am able to get on with the task of making money.

So here I am, waked up, shaken, standing still in this space when my old mind, which is by no means reconciled to my new mind, keeps nagging at me: "I need my sleep"; "I'll be a wreck if I don't get my sleep"; "I won't

be able to do my job properly"; "I can't do without my
sleep."

But I learned that I wasn't a wreck; instead, I was
revitalized. Yes, I fought against it, but some wonderful
intensity overcame the old mind, an expansion, a rising
up of the spirit, the consciousness. Merton and many
others have written of this awareness of entering a different dimension, being in a new world, yet being yourself, the same person. Merton said he felt as if the floor
had fallen out of his soul and he was free to go in and out
of infinity. He mentions that the mind was included,
and it, too, could enter "into the peace and harmony of
this infinite simplicity that had come to be born within
me."

Me, too, Lord. Here am I on Monday morning, more
myself than I have ever been. I am grateful to the
religious radicals of my century who broke the ice pack
and let me into the divine dimension with all my things,
assuring me that contemplative prayer is not for the
elite, but for anyone who seeks and desires. Those
religious radicals are the "hopers" who refuse to turn
the people of our century down. Nobody is too lost. I
am what I am and come with that *me* to rise up on
Monday morning and pray with Francis of Assisi at
Matins:

> You are the holy Lord God, who alone works
> marvels. You are powerful, you are full of majesty,
> you are the Most High. . . . You are what is
> good, all that is good, the supreme good, true
> and living Lord God. You are charity, love. You
> are wisdom. . . . You are humility. You are
> patience. . . . You are joy and gladness. You are
> justice and temperance. . . . You are all the
> wealth one can desire.
>
> *(Office of the Paters)*

A friend sent me a small paperback entitled *Bhakti-Yoga, The Yoga of Love and Devotion* by Swami Vivekananda. There I discovered a prayer very like the one said at Matins on Monday as part of the Office prayed with Saint Francis. It is in the section Shvetashvatar-Upanishad, VI:17-18.

> He is the Soul of the Universe; He is immortal: His is the Rulership; He is the All-knowing, the All-pervading, the Protector of the Universe, the Eternal Ruler. None else is there efficient to govern the world eternally.

Where my mind is, there my heart is, one person, and suddenly this one person praying with Francis of Assisi forgets it is Monday at dawn, because of the joy of connections!

But there is an exciting difference, too. Francis is not abstract—*his* holy Lord, the Soul of the Universe, is also *our* joy and gladness, our justice and temperance. The human relationship is essential. The prayers of Francis at the canonical hours point this up. Time is not an illusion; it is a touchstone. Certainly when I change my life's times to this different beat, everything in my life is different. Time is never heavy on my hands, and I never wish to kill time. Merton discovered that even after decades of living in this different time, the canonical hours never grew stale.

When he went to live alone in his hermitage, no one could check up on him, and he might have eased the disciplines. Instead he went farther *out*. He got up in icy dark at 2:15 A.M. Having to go crunching over the snow and dried corn husks, put down to keep the feet from slipping on the path to "the jakes," could be "a grievous shock." But he joked about physical discomforts.

"I have almost two hours to pray or read or think by myself and make up the night office."

That's it. You are all the wealth I can desire! Even on Monday.

Tuesday Morning at Lauds

Dawn. The moon is going down, and the little silver stars blink as if they are tired after the long night's shining. There is suspense in the air; everything is waiting. Then a bird begins to sing. It is Francis singing a canticle to the Maker of this new day:

Be praised, my Lord, for Sister Moon and the
    Stars—
In the heavens you make them bright and fair
    and precious.
Be praised, my Lord, for Brother Wind,
And for the air, for cloudy, fair, and every kind
    of weather,
Through which you give your creatures
    sustenance.

(Canticle of the Sun)

To be made mindful by my teacher, this morning, that it's a new world, the beginning of a new day, all things made new, begins my day on a note of goodness, no matter how bad things are with me. Thank you, Lord, for weather! I love weather, every kind of weather: the wind, the air, cloudy, fair. When I walk out, the dawn wind stirs the air, the air moves around me, stirs up my body and stirs up my soul. I pray that the wind stir inside me as well as outside. I pray for the soul's weather.

Blow, wind, freshen the heavy atmosphere inside my mind; stir up my old tired blood; breathe this good air, my soul.

"The Blessed Virgin Compared to the Air We Breathe," Gerard Manley Hopkins's poem, gives me a

deeper insight into Francis of Assisi and his praise for
the air. Hopkins describes the air as the "nursing element" on which we must draw and draw. He says it puts
him in mind "of her"—of Mary Immaculate—for we
are meant "to share Her life as life does air." For "we
are wound with mercy round and round as if with air."

Thomas Merton plays a variation on this theme in his
meditation entitled *Hagia Sophia*, which is a section of
his *Emblems of a Season of Fury*. He writes of the invisible
fecundity, the mysterious unity and integrity inherent
in all visible things, and calls this mysterious "Unity and
Integrity" (capitalizing the words), "Wisdom, the
Mother of all." He feels this mothering Wisdom rising
up "in wordless gentleness" and flowing out to him
"from the unseen roots of created being, welcoming me
tenderly, saluting me with indescribable humility."
Wisdom, Hagia Sophia, is Mary:

> The Blessed Virgin Mary is the one created being
> who enacts and shows forth in her life all that is
> hidden in Sophia. . . .   Thus her consent opens
> the door of created nature, of time, of history, to
> the Word of God.

There! That is why I am here this morning, Lord. I
want to go through that door; the door opened. *You*
came in; *I* can go out. Francis saw Mary as the mother of
Wisdom also, and what a spirit of logic there is in this,
for Jesus said, "I am the Way, the Truth, the Life"; so,
the "mother of Wisdom" is the phrase that most com-
pletely describes Mary.

Lauds. Right now I am walking in the wind, the dog is
prancing in the wind, his ears are blowing, his tail is
blowing, and I am reading the words for the canonical
hour and thinking: to make a space for God in my life,
right now! Mary made space for God very literally, in
her body, and out of her body. On Saturday, when

Francis of Assisi gives praise to Mary, he tells us at Vespers to think of the space she made both inside her body and out:

> We are our Lord's mothers when we carry him about in our heart and person by means of love and a clean and sincere conscience, and we give birth to him by means of our actions which should shine. . . .
>
> (Letter to All the Faithful)

The sun lifting up over the far horizon sends rays of light, the light that brings life, over this part of the earth. But the light has to go through air. If there is no air, there is no light, there is no life. Light must have air, just as we must have air, and Francis did not need scientific data to be made aware of this wonderful, essential-to-life phenomenon of light and air. Like Hopkins, he saw knowledge of this kind as mystical, and he compared Mary to the air carrying the light, the Light that is the Life; without air, the sun could not shine with life-givingness on our planet Earth and on our earthy selves.

The sun is one of the most demanding allegories of spirituality, which all peoples, of any or even no religious intuitions, recognized from the first. One year when I was living in New Mexico and walked out to pray at Lauds, I saw a Pueblo Indian father teaching his boy to go at dawn and stand in the open door and throw a pinch of cornmeal in the direction of the rising sun, affirming the coming of life and the role of sun and air bringing life. The sun, at the center, shines everywhere yet has no boundary. How I love that thought! There is no way I, or we, or anybody can keep the rays of the sun from getting into everyone's life; the sun is for everybody. And its shining does not empty it. No matter how much it radiates light, its radiating does not diminish it.

We do not need to be competitive about who gets
more sun!

I look up at the sky. As the sun rises, its light has a
purity like that of a glass of water, and I think of the
famous biochemist Lewis Thomas: "Taken all in all,"
he wrote, "the sky is a miraculous achievement." There
is a particular excitement in the mystical insights of the
twentieth-century scientists.

> The word "chance" does not serve to account well
> for structures of such magnificence. . . .   It
> breathes for us, and it does another thing for our
> pleasure.   Each day millions of meteorites fall
> against the outer limits . . . and are burned to
> nothing by the friction. Without this shelter, our
> surface would long since have become the pounded
> powder of the moon.

He compares the life-sustaining quality of the air to
bread and wine—to the religious sacrament, so mysterious, so mystical.

> Be praised, my Lord, for Sister Moon and the
>   Stars—
> In the heavens you make them bright and fair
>   and precious.

Without *You* there is no thing, no brightness, no fair-
ness. All things lose their value if nobody made them
and they are but an accident. But suppose creation is no
accident! The scientist Lewis Thomas says that the
word *chance* does not serve to account well for structures
of such magnificence.

Yet the word *chance* is the most popular word among
those who undertake to tell the story of the cosmos. I
was watching the television show entitled *Cosmos*—a
carefully, seriously prepared document for public television. The teacher and commentator was Professor

Carl Sagan, and how dogmatically, with a kind of nervous insistence, he pounded away on the theme of *chance*! The cosmos just happened, an accident, a chance combination of elements resulting from a big boom when a puff of hydrogen exploded.

Unlike the great modern scientists who are geniuses precisely because they are mystics—Einstein, Laing, Lovell, Buckminster Fuller—there is no room in Sagan's cosmos for openness, for leaving unanswered (because unanswerable in terms of our limited comprehension and vocabulary) the mystery of the origin of the universe.

Sir Bernard Lovell, Nobel Prize-winning physicist and professor of radio astronomy, writes that in the agelong search for deeper understanding of the universe

> the majority of new ideas have eventually transpired to be wrong, while philosophical concepts with little observational basis have emerged as correct.
>
> (*In the Center of the Immensities*)

He notes that science moves by way of *hypotheses* that can be wrong as often as right. They don't have to be right, for they are only starting points—like Columbus setting out to find India and discovering America.

This is how the human mind works, and it is how my mind works. I have to go through many wrong hypotheses, wrong hunches, mistaken attitudes, poor judgments. I have to keep trying to come clear. I can't just hunker down in wrong, mistaken hypotheses and refuse to go another step. There is something in the mind that wants to get things right, and must keep seeking.

Lewis Thomas says that the human brain alone has this extraordinary genius for getting things wrong, so as

to get something bigger and deeper right. It is a significant and paradoxical gift. But how hopeful! Especially
for me right now on this Tuesday at dawn. I can praise,
knowing that all my mistakes, my blunders, my stupidi-
ties, my unintelligent analyses of how to act and think
are just the weight lifting of the mind! And the soul.

The eternal verities, the philosophical concepts with
little "observational basis," remain the foundation
stones, in contrast to the scientific hypotheses that are
scaffolding only. The North Star knows the north even
when I don't, so that's what I steer by when my little
mind gets me off my course. I find my way by the North
Star, the philosophical concept, which in my case is religion: You, Lord, who make things, *you* make things
bright and fair and precious—without you all is vanity,
as Ecclesiastes laments. Lovell also notes that we con-
fuse knowledge with wisdom, though they are not the
same thing. The Information Age may not bring us
wisdom if we dissociate our search for knowledge from
the search for wisdom. Our knowledge about how to
make an atom bomb did not lead us to a deeper insight
into the nature of the universe but only increased our
will to self-destruction.

This morning I'm taking all the modern scientists
into my Praises because modern science is about the
moon and the stars and the air. Francis leads me into
modern science today as I praise the rising of the sun.
I'm including a writer I've just discovered. His name is
Morris Berman, and he writes that the scientific revolution that began with the Renaissance in Western culture
destroyed a whole dimension of the human imagination:

> Before this revolution, people felt the world was a
> harmonious place, however dangerous and incom-
> pletely understood. . . . Rocks, trees, rivers and
> clouds were all seen as wondrous, alive, and human

beings felt at home in this environment. The Cosmos was a place of *belonging*. . . . Everything was
alive, spirited, infused with the grace of God.
                                    (*The Reenchantment of the World*)

But the scientific revolution showed us that knowledge could be used to make money. We love money.
Knowledge as a tool of material influence was more
attractive than knowledge as a tool of wisdom. Our
problem is that with the former we brought ourselves
and our earth toxic lakes, mercury-contaminated
oceans, dying birds and marine life, and a stockpile of at
least fifty thousand nuclear warheads. We are just
beginning to perceive that the amazing knowledge
opened to us in the seventeenth-century scientific
revolution must now be used as a tool of wisdom.

When I put the leash on the dog this morning, he
stuck his cold, wet nose in my ear. He seemed to be
saying, "Up and out!" And we went out on a run. All
the houses looked humble and very temporary, not built
of solid stones and great timbers, but as modern houses
are built. When those of us who live in the desert go
away to escape the summer heat, we come back to find
great sand dunes rising up on what was once the patio.
In my little green book, Francis's words for Compline
on Saturday are, "The spirit of the Lord applies itself to
humility and patience."

I'm not patient with the Information Age and resent
the human diminishment; any machine can do better
than we do. Yet we humans, despite our insistence on
our nothingness, are the power brokers, and though we
may be but handfuls of dust, we're awesome, endowed
with a knowledge that can, dispraising, do foreseeable
ruin to this cosmos. Or? We can praise!

The Bible says we are made in his image. We can
think a thought, we can put the thought into an act, and

we can change life on earth. The prayer at Compline, the seventh and last of the canonical hours, is said at night. The humility and patience that my teacher enjoins speak to our inner dark. I try to learn to be patient and humble not only in my darkness, but with the hope for better light, more clarity of understanding —to be patient and humble not in order to annihilate my ego nor to "naught" my *self*, but in order to enlighten the self, to light up my ego.

Moon, quarter moon, you are hanging low like an empty cradle in the western sky. Where is the little man who used to lie in that cradle?

I think of David, the Old Testament poet, who asked so many questions. As he gazed at the heavens and the works of the Lord, he cried out how glorious is the Lord's name, and in the same breath asked, What is man that you should care about him?

And he knew why he was asking. He knew how bad he was, a passionately willful, violent, sexually headstrong and insensitive-to-the-hurts-of-others human being. Yet he knew he was not thereby diminished. With all his degradation, he humbly stood up and sang *loud* the praises of the Lord.

There is a great blaze of light, and the sun breaks over the land. I recall the Indian boy at dawn in New Mexico tossing the pinch of cornmeal in the direction of the rising sun, affirming, praising the sun rising on a new day to bring life yet another day to our planet Earth. And my mind connects it with another happening, also in New Mexico: the detonation of the first atom bomb near Alamogordo on July 16, 1945. I read the words of the woman physicist and her husband who drove to a mountaintop to see that show, the greatest show on earth. "A hellish light," she and her husband cried as they saw the mountaintops, the crevasses, the cliffs blaze with a light they could only describe as malevolent. "It looks like Doomsday."

The man known to the world as "the father of the atomic bomb" had named the test area, the Alamogordo Bombing Range, Trinity. He said he had been thinking of John Donne's *Holy Sonnets*:

> Batter my heart, three person'd God, for, you
> As yet but knock, breathe, shine, and seek to
> mend.
> That I may rise and stand, o'erthrow me and
> bend
> Your force to break, blow, burn, and make me
> new.

Almost all the scientists involved in the exploding of the atom bomb, the first ever made in the history of our species, felt themselves at spiritual risk. It was a mystical thing. No one tried to explain it, but J. Robert Oppenheimer used the word *Trinity* almost as a magical word of prayer—not so much to pray for the success of the work in hand, the making of what they were making, as to reverse the potential for evil. When the bomb was exploded, the scientists took shelter in trenches, and those who recovered first looked through dark squares of colored glass at a huge ball of fire, like the sun at close range, rising from the desert in a "swirling inferno of reds and oranges and yellows." Oppenheimer, remembering a line from the Hindu *Bhagavad Gita*, murmured: "I am become death, the shatterer of worlds."

I think the intuition to use words like *Trinity*, to speak in terms of heaven and hell, to quote Donne, to recall lines from the *Bhagavad Gita*, is an act of prayer. They didn't get down on their knees and say the Lord's Prayer or make an Act of Contrition, but they spontaneously cried out words of prayer. There is a life-preserving instinct deep in us that makes us pray, makes us try

to right things by giving a "hellish light" a name that
can transform hell into heaven, like the name *Trinity*. In
the depths of each one of us, believer or unbeliever, is
this knowledge that the Word started us on the path of
God, of Truth, and we turn to the Word—the spiritual
Word; they call it a mantra in Eastern religions, a prayer
in Western religions. If there is no humility in us, it is an
attempt at magic; if there is humility, it is praise to God
for an extraordinary opening into a kind of knowledge
that we must then choose to use either for wisdom or for
death.

Since that July. day in 1945 on the New Mexico
desert, after the first nuclear event, we have suffered a
break in time. Nothing is the same, as if the innocence
of time, our element through which we go to Infinity,
had been raped. All the options turned into one option,
destruction. How can I say Lauds after *that*, teacher?
Would David continue his psalms of praise? Maybe he
would, undoubtedly he did, for he had murdered his
best friend in order to get away with his friend's wife.
But can I see my own personal destructiveness in the
same class as Hiroshima?

We don't understand. I don't mean about the atom,
or nuclear physics, or the quantum theory. I mean we
don't understand our destructive passion, the intensity
of our will to annihilate one another, our earth, our
cosmos. We don't understand why we're this way, and
that destroys our faith in God. I don't understand the
Holocaust in the era of the Nazis, yet when I think of
what we Americans did to Hiroshima, I think of that
event ("the first controlled chain reaction") as another
facet of the same hard diamond embedded in our
minds, with its baleful light turning and turning, the
diamond *we* made. This was what we made when we

made light. To destroy life is all we can think to do with the kind of light *we* made.

When God made light he made life.

Every element has its opposite. The fire of love is not the same fire as the fire of hate; the light that brings life is not the same light as the light that brings death. I recall the film documentaries of the bombing of Hiroshima, how everything was fragmented, melted down, all shapes were destroyed, and how the realization hit me: "This is the meaning of chaos—all shapes are destroyed, and only blobs of senselessness remain." It seemed a vision of pure hate.

The shapes of love are always tending toward wholeness, health, the harmonious bringing together of spirit and matter. Contemplative prayer is the loving seeking of wholeness, sound humanity, genuine human dignity. In the depths of our society there is this constant stirring. We keep trying to rise up but are weighed down by the assaults on sound humanity, on genuine human dignity, on the culture of thought, ethics, imagination that we humans have loved into life out of the word given by God.

Why do I have to remember and to bring these things to the divine encounter? This morning I'd like to pray without memory, take a respite from human iniquity and my own failures that are part of all this. Why think about it? All I really want is to pray, to forget, to be united with God in a cloud of unknowing exaltation. I want to get *out* of my time and *into* the purity and timelessness of spiritual life, but I'm not permitted. Why?

I think of Alfred Delp, the young Jesuit priest executed by the Nazis. He didn't want to die; he had work to do. But a mentally deranged society regarded his kind of work, the love and assistance to Christ's poor, as a threat. In reading his prison meditations, I am struck by his remark that our loss of sound humanity makes us

incapable of making contact with God, even incapable
of ordinary understanding.

The whole human condition is part of who I am and
why I am here, and I can't cop out. My species' history
through the eons is part of me now and must also be
brought to my prayer of Lauds, along with my lack of
understanding. Strangely, when I pray and praise God,
a little stir takes place in my darkness, and I understand
more profoundly than I did before what Saint John of
the Cross is trying to tell me:

> To attain union with God, a person should advance
> neither by understanding nor by the support of his
> own experience, nor by feeling or by imagination,
> but by belief in God's being.
>
> (*The Collected Works*)

We are standing still now, the dog and I. He is
absorbed in the musky scent of a mesquite bush, and I
am absorbed in the canonical hour of Lauds, which
turns me from my own modes and makes me enter on a
way that is not my way.

> Be praised, my Lord, for Sister Moon and the
>   Stars—
> In the heavens you make them bright and fair
>   and precious.
> Be praised, my Lord, for Brother Wind,
> And for the air, for cloudy, fair, and every kind
>   of weather,
> Through which you give your creatures
>   sustenance.
>
> (*Canticle of the Sun*)

A sudden wind has come up with the sun. It blows
away the darkness, but for a moment I have seen how it
can be both the Dark Night and the coming of day.

Wednesday Morning at Lauds

Francis of Assisi was not a medium. He was not even a seer. He did not look into the seeds of time and foretell which seeds would grow and which would die. He had no foreknowledge of the first controlled chain reaction and the evil light of destruction and fallout, which human beings would devise like children playing with matches in a dry wood. Nor could he, by precognition or intuition, have any knowledge of the hard rain that would fall on the humbly unresisting earth, the rain that came down after the weeks and months of explosion of dirty bombs in the clear pure ozone of the New Mexico desert, indiscriminately killing sheep, horses, and children.

It is nevertheless eerie to get up on Wednesday at dawn and discover that Lauds is a canticle of purification and joyful praise of renewal. On Wednesday everything that died on Tuesday is reborn—a new dawn, another chance.

> Be praised, my Lord, for Sister Water,
> Most useful is she, and humble, and precious and
>   chaste.
> Be praised, my Lord, for Brother Fire,
> By which you light up the night;
> And it is fair and gay, and hardy and strong.
>   (*Canticle of the Sun*)

Still here? Yes, Lord, still here.

I was reading the journal of George Fox, the founder of the Society of Friends, when I came on these words:

I saw the infinite love of God. I saw also that there was an ocean of darkness and death; but an infinite ocean of light and love flowed over the ocean of darkness. In that also I saw the infinite love of God, and I had great openings.

I felt that I too had great openings. An infinite ocean of light and love flows over the ocean of darkness, but it is not vague, dreamy, spiritual! Francis of Assisi means real water. Sister Water, the water I am drinking from this glass right now, on Wednesday morning, as I take my niacin pill, is flowing over my hand from the tap. The infinite ocean of light and love, the water of life, flows over this tap water: the waters from the well of life, "the river of life, rising from the throne of God and of the Lamb and flowing crystal clear down the middle of the city."

Contemplative prayer is inseparable from life and from the creativity of aliveness. Eknath Easwaran, Buddhist teacher of contemplation, said to me:

My approach to the scriptures is entirely on this basis: that they are practical manuals to the art of living and the truths in them are verifiable by anyone prepared to undergo a certain ethical and mental discipline.

He paused, was silent for a few minutes, then went on:

Meditation develops the most precious capacity that the human being can have, the capacity to turn anger into compassion, fear into courage, hatred into love.

This Wednesday morning I am thinking of that. To turn my anger into compassion is a new chance, a new birth. Give me another chance, God. A new dawn.

This is the miracle of meditation, this is my motivation
as one who seeks the prayers of contemplation: not to
see visions, not to hear voices, but to purify my heart, to
turn my anger into compassion, my fear into courage,
my hatred into love! To be born again this morning so I
can honestly speak the praises of Lauds, to go through
the water and the fire.

Lectio Divina

Saint Benedict of Nursia is called the patriarch of Western monks. He lived from 480 to about 543, and in that
brief time, a bit over sixty years, he put together the
rule of monastic life that was to serve as a model for
religious orders henceforth. He was a humanist and
believed in spiritual reading, *lectio divina.* The canonical
hours (the divine office, as he called it) was his doing,
and what he put together fourteen centuries ago is still
being sung all over the world. He wished the monks "so
to sing the psalms that mind and voice may be in harmony." But he did not want mindless chanting, and he
set forth certain standards for time spent imbuing the
mind with mental and spiritual values, through reading.
He required his abbot to be a man of learning. As for
himself, he devoted "an average of four hours daily to
lectio divina." The monastery was not to be a place only
of pious meditation: "The monks of the West gave
themselves to humane as well as sacred studies—monastic studies encompassed the culture" (Dom Justin
McCann, *St. Benedict*).

Gilbert K. Chesterton said: "What St. Benedict
stored, St. Francis scattered."

Francis scattered the seeds of divine learning, and
this morning as I am reading his canticle verse praising
water and fire, many variations on this theme enter my
mind. I think of the life that water brings, in a spiritual
sense. When my soul is parched, reading the lines of a

psalm, or a chapter in a novel by Willa Cather, or a poem by John Berryman is water, and I am refreshed. Such reading, for me, is *lectio divina.* And when I think of all the arts—sculpture, music, painting, philosophy —the fire, the divine fire, lights up the night, and it is fair and gay and hardy and strong!

So this morning I praise all those who awaken the spirit, by evoking the fire of life and the water of compassion: The joy of heart speaking to heart comes when I remember that Dorothy Day's favorite quotation was from the novelist Fyodor Dostoyevsky: "Love in action is a harsh and dreadful thing compared to love in dreams." From this she took her scriptural lesson.

Now, in the twentieth century, we have achieved the right to read the poets and novelists as part of our spiritual grounding. But in the nineteenth century and the first third of the twentieth, artists, poets, and novelists above all were looked upon with suspicion, as sinners luring readers into sin. Only those who used their creative talents to describe saccharine and pietistic lives, for purely religious propaganda, could escape denunciation and censorship. When the famous sculptor Jacob Epstein sculptured Christ as a man with Semitic features and a suffering look, instead of the handsome, fair-haired Englishman seen on calendars, he was denounced and bitterly condemned.

Novelists like François Mauriac and Graham Greene who wrote novels about religious conflict within the human heart were condemned as "amateur theologians"; and both expressed their feelings that they were sinners for having been given the gift of novel-writing! Max Jacob, the French surrealist poet and convert Jew, was a true contemplative, and his friend André Billy wrote of him: "He longed to direct his energies, talents, everything solely to religious life, and asked himself what he should do—become a monk? A priest?" But everyone assured him he had no vocation, and he believed them. How could he have a vocation when he wrote satiric poetry, bitter and mocking, like the religious paintings of Rouault? When Max Jacob died in the prison camp of the Nazis, at Drancy, Jacques Maritain wrote of him that his conversion to Christianity "shed its rays on modern poetry."

Saint Francis of Assisi is always described as anti-intellectual, but at the same time—paradoxically—he is called "the father of the Italian Renaissance." He was a first-rate poet, and a first-rate poet cannot be anti-intellectual; Saint Francis only rejected a particular kind of rationalism and pedantic fraud that passed for intellectuality. But Francis knew the difference; he would recognize the difference between the poet Dante and the IBM word processor. Francis was not a simple person.

When one goes beyond the usual romantic clichés about Saint Francis, one discovers a person who, for all his transparent attractiveness, is complex to the point of enigma. . . . The life of Saint Francis triggered an outpouring of religious and aesthetic creativity of such magnitude that it is now commonplace among scholars to reckon his influence as basic in catalyzing the Italian Renaissance.
(Cunningham and Stock,
Saint Francis of Assisi)

Some years ago when Kenneth Clark was narrating a beautiful television production entitled *Civilisation*, he described Francis of Assisi as the father of Western culture.

The great variety of my spiritual reading enriches my prayerlife and helps me rise above my own banality and triviality, so that when I get up on Wednesday to say the prayer of Lauds with Saint Francis, it is never mechanical.

I think of the Russian novelist Dostoyevsky—how he
loved Christ. He was obsessed with innocent suffering,
particularly the suffering of children. He made lists of
battered and sexually abused children and called out the
viciousness and the shame to the whole world of readers. Yet, for him, Christ would make everything good;
good and joyful, turning our weeping into singing. Dostoyevsky, whose life was so terrible, in poverty and sick-
ness, death and disaster! He praised Sister Water in the
morning when he got up to wash his face, and he
thought of Christ and how Christ takes the humble
water of our earth and uses it for our spiritual joy:

> Cana of Galilee, the first miracle. Ah, that miracle!
> Ah, that sweet miracle! It was not men's grief but
> their joy Christ visited. He worked His first miracle
> to help men's gladness.
>
> *(The Brothers Karamazov)*

I had never thought of the first miracle, when Christ
took common water and made wine, as the miracle of
bringing joy to our human celebrations. Now it is
always in my deep meditations, thanks to Dostoyevsky.
Does Saint Francis know Dostoyevsky on that immortal
plane where all times are simultaneous and all the
immortals come together "as peers"? They are so alike
in my thoughts. Both were filled with the fiery knowledge that Christ came "to help men's gladness." This is
what Francis means by all his Praises: Christ came to
help our gladness. "Be praised, my Lord, for Brother
Fire"—for the fire of love. It creates, it lights us up, it
makes life worth living; we are helped to be glad in the
midst of so much that is sad.

The famous story about the dinner Saint Francis gave
for Saint Clare is always part of my thoughts when I
praise the fire that does not destroy but creates. Saint

Clare came with a companion to share a meal with Francis and the brothers. Francis prepared the meal; then they sat down on the earth to pray, the brothers ringed around them, and Francis began to speak:

> And with the first dish St. Francis began to discourse of God so sweetly, so loftily, and so wondrously that a bounteous measure of divine grace descended upon them and they were all rapt in God. And being thus ravished, with eyes and hands lifted up to heaven, the men of Assisi and of Bettona, and the men of the country round about, beheld St. Mary of the Angels and the whole friary and the wood that was around about it brightly flaming; and it seemed as 'twere a great fire that was devouring the church and the friary and the wood together: wherefore the men of Assisi, verily believing that everything was in flames, ran down thither with great haste to quench the fire. But when they came to the friary and found nothing burning, they entered within and beheld St. Francis with St. Clare and all their companions seated around that humble table and rapt in the contemplation of God. Wherefore they understood that truly the fire had not been a material fire, but a divine fire which God had miraculously made to appear in order to show forth and signify the fire of divine love wherewith the souls of these holy friars and holy nuns did burn; and they departed with great consolation in their hearts and with holy edification.
>
> (*The Little Flowers & the Life of St. Francis with The Mirror of Perfection*)

Heaven breaks in—not as a spook or ghostly emanation, not because everybody is sitting around holding hands as in a séance; heaven breaks in like light, real light, light that can set fire to people, the way sunlight coming through crystal, through a fragment of glass, ignites when held over wood or paper.

I don't expect or even ask to have this experience when I pray. When I got up this morning to praise with Saint Francis, I only wanted to begin this new day on an upbeat note, to give the day a good send-off.

Yet I am, I must admit, elated when I think of those whose love of God has set them on fire, and I feel something good in my life just knowing about them and standing up at dawn to be in their company. If I shine only because their light is reflected from all the dark windows, including my dark window, I am glad to shine with reflected light. The light and love that illuminates their lives shines through them and illuminates me— through them! So I read them, and their new radical spirituality, blazing up inside, shines into me. Through them I share the contemplative experience, even though I am not a gifted contemplative. I do not need to be one who has been given the special gift. There is a gift of sharing that all of us have. There is the wonderfulness of being a listener. I can listen to music without being able to play any instrument, without knowing a note. I can listen to opera, I can listen to and delight in the singing of the singer, though I cannot sing a note, and though in truth if I try to sing, everyone at once leaves.

Thanks to matter, thanks to my materiality, thanks to God entering into matter, I can partake of the life of contemplation and share the insights of the mystics. Matter makes this sharing possible. The way God comes to my soul, by way of the light that shines through another, is possible only because of our materiality, which is so responsive—matter continually responds, like a sounding board. Thanks to the body, this thing, this *cosa*, we can give each other the kiss of *nada!* Of *nada?* Yes, nothing, meaning spirit; that is, not matter.

Close Encounters

This paradox cannot be explained, just as Bernard of Clairvaux could not explain how he knew when God was present but could simply say he recognized God's presence by the movement of his heart. It burned within him.

One night, on television, I watched the film *Close Encounters of the Third Kind.* It was the second time I was seeing it, and there was no diminishing of the excitement I felt that these ordinary, everyday people, in the midst of their ordinary, everyday lives, were given to experience something *good* coming from another dimension of the cosmos. Beneficent voyagers entered their lives briefly. The sky was filled with beautiful lights, and a vast starry constellation was their spaceship, armored with nothing but light and goodwill. All those given to witness this were burned. Their faces were burned on one side, the side turned to the sky, so that they had a bad case of sunburn, or looked as if they had. The most moving thing, however, was that they were burning up inside, fired by something new, radically new, beyond their ability to explain to those who had not seen what they had seen.

This morning it seems natural to praise that film! It is part of my Lauds, for I think, "Yes, we too have an inkling of that burning love; we too try to symbolize and communicate it in a contemporary way, and bring others the awareness."

Even if you never read the canticles of Francis or the songs of Bernard of Clairvaux, if you pay attention to what is sometimes said to us by the writers, the poets, the filmmakers of our own times, you know it isn't something that belongs in the past. The fire of love is for us

too—in our language. My prayers make a continuity
each morning as I bring my own time, with the language
and imagery of my time, to this ancient canonical hour
of prayer.

The Lord said he was giving us something *new*, and in
response I dare to accept the challenge and bring *him*
something new: *me* and my time, whatever it is, such as it
is! And for these gifts I am bringing, so ridiculous, like a
child bringing a handful of pebbles, I want only one
thing in return—a kiss on the mouth!

The *Bhakti-Yoga, The Yoga of Love and Devotion* also
uses the language of human love to describe divine love.
In the *sutras*, the vocabulary of human romantic passion
is used to describe mystical love, even speaking of the
kiss on the lips, as Saint Bernard does.

> For one kiss of Thy lips, O Beloved! One who has
> been kissed by Thee has his thirst for Thee increas-
> ing forever, all his sorrows vanish, and he forgets
> all things except Thee alone.

The commentator Swami Vivekananda then
remarks:

> Aspire after that kiss of the Beloved, that touch of
> His lips which makes the Bhakta mad, which makes
> of man, a god. To him, who has been blessed with
> such a kiss, the whole of nature changes, worlds
> vanish, suns and moons die out, and the universe
> itself melts away into that one infinite ocean of
> love. That is the perfection of the madness of love.

I am amazed and elated every time these connections
are revealed to my mind. Everything joins together and
throws more light on all we take for granted. Seeing
relationships brings new understanding of similarities.
I am also aware of the differences, and it seems to me
that we, in all our different approaches to God, have

been given different insights to fill out what our simplistic minds cannot comprehend. The infinite becomes personal; the personal enters into the infinite. Yet I know that in the Christian mystic's experience, the personal does not *become* the infinite, but enters into it and is somehow totally embraced, yet does not lose anything. I will still be *me*.

The kiss that makes the one who loves God forget all things is not unknown to those Old Testament Jews who in the New Testament went up the mountain with Christ and saw the Transfiguration. That sight made Peter cry out, "Lord, let's stay here and make three tents!"

They were longing to stay on the mountain, so rapt in the "madness of love" that neither earth nor nature mattered any more. They wanted to forget "all things except Thee alone." In this context they were like the Bhaktas (Hindus who practice the intense love of God), who, experiencing "the perfection of the madness of love," were utterly carried away, never to return. The apostles never wanted to return either, but Jesus would not let them stay on the mountain.

I often think of Christ making them go down the mountain, back into the troubles of their times. Christ's kiss does not make the mystic a "god" for whom the world vanishes and the universe melts away into the infinite ocean of love. The kiss of Christ is a paradox of Love, for the mystic is, by that kiss, sealed *to* the world! The kiss of Christ enables the Christian mystic to go forth and pick up the world and kiss it on the mouth, give *it* the kiss of Christ. Francis of Assisi did it. He kissed the mouth of the diseased human being. And I think of those in my own time, like Mother Teresa in India. She is the best known, but there are many like her. The kiss of Christ on the mouth sends the Christian mystic into the center of materiality—this is *dis-*

equilibrium. It is what throws me off balance, for my prayer at dawn is surely going to send me into the center of my world. How can I keep the two things in balance?

This is the work. I am learning that the vision of Saint Francis is not abstract, not the vision of the transcendent God dwelling in eternity. It is the overwhelming real confrontation of "God who is" in the immediate now of everyday reality.

My everyday reality is a place. It is right here wherever I am, and the laws of this place, the institutions, and all the structures, without which I could hardly get through this day, are part of my reality.

The water and the fire are holy. I have to carry the water in my little bowl, and I have to carry the fire, too —and bring into this new morning, this Wednesday morning, these gifts: Sister Water and Brother Fire, and the person who is the carrier, *me.*

Thursday Morning at Lauds

I wake up in the darkness, and worries, anxieties, resentments pour into my mind. This is Thursday, I remind myself. It is time for Lauds. "Fill us at daybreak with your kindness, that we may shout for joy and gladness all our days" (Ps. 90:12-13). The words of the psalm make me even more aware that I am mad at everybody this morning. Fill me with your kindness, teacher, because of myself I have none. I am mad at myself and at my supervisor. I am mad at the political scene, because politicians assure me that the rich are doing fine, even richer this year than last, though I am poorer—at least be happy for the rich! I am mad at the tired clerk in the supermarket who barked at me for coming into the store too close to closing time.

> Be praised, my Lord, for our
>   sister Mother Earth,
> Who sustains and guides us,
> And brings forth fruits of
>   many kinds, with many-
>   colored flowers and grass.
>
> *(Canticle of the Sun)*

Fill me with your kindness, you who make things, you who make love to us with all these things. Fill me with your kindness, Lord, for there's none to spare in my heart this morning, and though I will say the Praises for Thursday at Lauds with Saint Francis, because it is what I promised my teacher, I am really not in the mood.

I look out the window, and it seems that all the years of my life are part of that wintry scene. No fruit nor flowers grow out there. The patch of grass is frozen, brown. It is a bleak darkness.

But anyway, it's Thursday, I tell myself. Cheer up! Tomorrow is Friday, thank God, the end of another workweek. But this reminds me of all the tensions the workweek has brought so far, and it isn't over yet. I start running toward the mistakes that lie in the hours ahead, running to live my unhappiness before its time.

Stop now! Be still, be here, be present where you are, right now, this moment. Step into this space. Just stand in this space outside of time. Be still, and just be where you are. Where am I? At this moment this is where I am, in the space called Lauds, standing here looking out the window, and I call my prayer *Praise for a New Day.* A new dawn is beginning, and the darkness covers the earth out there because everything is waiting for me to start singing.

A dim silvery band is vibrating there in the eastern sky, cutting across the darkness, like an obscured beam of light cutting across a dark gray sea. Obscured, but still the light is there, though seen dimly through the clouds. It is getting lighter moment by moment, and as the sky grows lighter, the life of the earth appears, evoked from the darkness. The dim rays touch the tree outside my window, and it takes shape. All night the tree was there, but in the darkness it might as well not have been there, for I could not see it. The tree waited in the dark for the light to shine on it and make it visible.

Here I am, too, waiting for the light to give me shape, make me visible. I would like to be as still and patient as this tree—waiting, trusting that the light will surely come again this morning.

The light is stronger now and moves all over the tree, into the branches, into the very center of the tree, and as it slides up and down the trunk, suddenly I see all the

wounds of this great tree. It is old. The outside show of
dark green branches and leaves is a brave covering. But
now that the tree is exposed, I see that it has suffered,
that years have done things to it. At the heart of the
tree are dead branches, clumps of dead branches. The
tree is an old woman who has lived a long time and has
experienced much death. She carried the death close to
her heart. The branches are green with leaves that
cover the suffering, but now the wintry light reveals
what she has kept hidden. This old tree is still growing,
carrying her whole life of tree-ness, all she has lived
through. Scarred, holding on to broken branches, she
keeps on growing, carrying her dead branches along
with the living, still reaching up, still lifting her
branches to the high airy spaces of sky.

The dark green leaves look strong and tough; this
tree is not of a species that loses its leaves in winter.
Tree, what is your name? Are you an ash? Perhaps you
are related to the great ash of Norse mythology, Yggdrasill. Listen, Tree, you are so old yet so alive, you
must be Yggdrasill. Yggdrasill symbolizes the universe,
the great ash whose roots extend all over the world. I
will tell you who you are, Tree, in case you don't know.
At the root of Yggdrasill is the spring of water that is the
source of wisdom, and this is how you grow: you drop
your seed from the pod into the earth, and there in the
earth the seed waits through two cold winters.

I look in my little green book to see the connection
between the seed of the ancient ash, the two cold winters, and *me* standing here at Lauds. Here is the connection: It is in the prayer for Lauds that Saint Francis sings
on Saturday morning. On Saturday Francis praises the
Lord for "our brother the death of the body" because
"the second death shall do no harm." So we must stay in
the earth through two cold winters? Does it mean that if
I can make it through the winter of my storms, of anger,

hate, greed, jealousy, selfishness, then that is the first
death? And so? The second death, the body's death, can
do no harm to me? I will have come through the first
winter! The second winter brings the resurrection,
the awakening to a new life. Yes, I can make the
connection.

When the light of the second spring touches the
earth, the seed drinks up the water that comes down
through the loam. It swells and splits, then puts out two
roots; one goes down, the other up. The root that goes
down goes deep into the earth and fixes itself with tiny
claws, holding tight, holding the growing tree fast for a
century, even for a thousand years.

The redwood trees of California have outlived many
species of animals, survived cosmic upheavals on our
planet. In Yosemite's Tuolumne Grove a giant sequoia
had grown for two thousand years, carrying upward
such strange beauty in its powerful branches that the
viewer could not believe how its struggle to rise up in
sunlight and air despite awesome body blows would
result in such strength and beauty. Its immense
branches were terribly twisted, some were long dead,
the trunk was scarred by lightning blasts. Yet it continually put forth new young growth, new green. It was a
Blake-tree, a poetic tree, a parable. People called it the
Leaning Tower Tree because it had never grown per-
fectly straight during its two thousand years on earth.
But, though leaning, it was magnificent and gave life to
creatures: Birds nested in its branches, insects ate its
bark. It filled the air with resinous fragrance, and fami-
lies and children picnicked in its shade. It survived
blizzards, frightful winters, yet each spring, despite the
new scars where branches were broken close to the
heart, it kept growing. It did not go down under the
weight of winter snows; it did not go down blasted by
summer lightning.

One very still April day when there was not a breath
of wind, the great tree went over. The earth shook, and
the sound of the tree's dying vibrated through the forest. The shattered trunk showed the bright red heart-
wood. The root that went down into the heart had held
fast for two thousand years and then let go. The root
that went up never let go; only when the roothold failed
did the tree fall.

Tree outside my window, you are not an ash. The ash
loses its leaves in winter. But most trees and plants
embody this spiritual metaphor: a root that goes down,
called a descending axis or radicle, and a root that goes
up, called an ascending axis, rising up into a shoot, a
stem, a trunk, seeking air and light. Everything about
you is like a teaching, a parable; for instance, your chronology—the way your growth is inscribed physically on
your body. You grow in circles; the years are all circles;
visibly, inside, you keep a record of time.

That should be like our chronology. We too should
grow in circles—not in cycles, not returning forever
and ever to how we used to be, to our old habits, our old
ways of thinking, but in circles that spiral upward. How
strange that a root should know to go *up*, to go against
the gravity pull! That was the root that carried minerals
and food to the growing tree and kept on rising against
the pull of the earth, drawn by the light and the pull
toward the sky that was even stronger than the pull of
the earth. But it could not survive without the roothold.
Francis calls earth not "mother" but "sister Mother
earth."

Be praised, my Lord, for our
sister Mother Earth,
Who sustains and guides us. . . .

Earth is our roothold that sustains and guides us but
also kills us. Earth is not my mother; she is my older

sister. Earth is flawed, as we are. Earth suffers convul-
sions, she is split, has a split personality, is cruel, violent,
destructive, yet beautiful, good, creative, capable of
exaltation and despair, just as we are. And we are in this
work of redemption together; we are together in this
task of prayer, this work given us—to love all things, to
love earth and all that lives on it, and ourselves into
heaven. Saint Paul tells us that the whole earth groans
and waits for redemption. The redemption of the earth
depends on us. That is the "new" thought, the "new"
spirituality" born in our age. Francis knew this time
would come. It has come.

A cattle rancher in Nebraska, interviewed on television about the sufferings of the farmers, spoke of greed,
foreclosures, loss of a lifetime's work. He told of the
hardships from nature's furies, the floods, the droughts.
Then he said in a dry, commonsense voice:

> Pretending that the farm problem, or any ques-
> tion, can be solved independently or apart from the
> central question of the arms race and planet sur-
> vival is like doctoring a tooth on judgment day—all
> the problems have become one, and all living
> things have become brothers and sisters. Farmers
> cannot farm, preachers cannot preach, teachers
> teach or living things live apart from national and
> international political decisions. All are tied to
> survival.

Francis of Assisi lived eight centuries ago, and this
rancher in Nebraska occupies a part of the earth I will
never see. The three of us will never meet. Yet we are
here together now in this space, the space of Lauds.
Here at dawn, praising my sister mother earth, I am
with them; we are together in the spirit of loving and
caring for our world and trying to follow the Christ-
ideal of changing our selfishness into self-giving.

My mind is stretched, my spirit is expanded, by this broader vision that has altered my understanding of salvation, of redemption. When I get up to pray at dawn with my green book open to the canticles of Francis, my spirit is not in accord with the nineteenth century's pietistic and devotional emphasis on my own salvation, on *me*, to save *myself*. In those times the earth was rejected. It was called "the world" wherein Christ said he had no part. We are confused creatures. It takes a long time for light to filter through our darkness.

Thursday is the day the Church recalls Christ going up to Jerusalem and together with his friends, in the upper room, taking bread, breaking it, and giving each one a piece to eat; then taking wine and blessing it and giving each to drink from the same cup. The bread came from the wheat of the earth; the wine from the juice of the grapes. It was a powerful drama of wholeness he enacted that evening at supper. And the words! They were spiritual words we have never understood and will grasp only after we have shuffled off this mortal coil: "This is my Body. This is my Blood."

It is mind-shattering to think of *eating* Christ—for us, who love to eat! Our "nature" is to devour all that lives, to devour the very earth greedily. We see ourselves in all those nature documentaries on TV: the Wildlife Series, the National Geographic series, the Nova series. And one thing is emphasized, above all other characteristics of living things: Eat, eat, eat! The fish are swallowing other fish, the birds are eating all the worms, some insects are eating one another's eggs, some are eating one another; the beasts are devouring one another. Every creature, including us, is devouring everything in sight. Francis of Assisi saw the natural state and sat down on the earth to eat ashes!

But he knew that while all other creatures must live by constantly feeding off one another, we human beings'

are different. We have been made mindful, endowed
with intellect, the gift of mindfulness. It is our light, and
by this light we are made aware of how different we are
from all other creatures, and how that difference is the
difference of responsibility. We, with the godly gift, are
responsible for our sister mother earth and for all that
lives; we can nurture and care for our earth and all that
lives, or we can devour and destroy. God gave *us* dominion! Typically we didn't understand the word *dominion*;
we thought its significance was not nurturing and
responsibility but "All this is for *me*!"

Greedy beyond all the other creatures, who live
according to their natures and eat what they must, we,
who live on another plane that includes spirit, can dis-
tort the meaning of life. We still take it for granted that
the world and all things in it are ours to exploit ruth-
lessly. How many countless species of creatures, so
imaginatively created by the Creator of all things, have
we mindlessly eradicated! We "waste" the earth. The
gangster word *waste*, meaning "kill," accurately tells
how we have understood dominion. The philosopher
Joseph Wood Krutch once said, in a lecture, "If man
destroys a work of man he's called a vandal; if man
destroys a work of God he's called a sportsman."

When I meditate on my scene, this earth, my sister
mother earth, it is even more beautiful to me now than
when I was not as mindful of earth's need for me as of
my need for it. And the thought comes to me that the
self-naughting enjoined by all the great spiritual teachers must be tied into the idea of *responsibility*. When I
seek to destroy my greed, to turn my selfishness into
self-giving, then I see that *nada*—making nothing of the
self—is essential to the preservation of *cosa*!

But this is a "new" insight even for the saints. One
summer, on a retreat at the Cenacle Retreat House in
Carmichael, California, I was given a mimeographed

lesson from the *Spiritual Exercises* of Ignatius of Loyola. There I read that Saint Ignatius says:

> All things on the face of the earth are created for man to help him in attaining the end for which he is created. . . . Man is to make use of them in as far as they help him in the attainment of his end, and he must rid himself of them in as far as they prove a hindrance to him.

This teaching leaves me too much on my own, passing judgments that are beyond me. What might appear as a hindrance to my spiritual growth may actually be the obstacle that is forcing me to break out of old habits of thinking, forcing me to break open new visions of connections between *me* and all creation, and hence new responsibilities.

Two Roots

The sun lights up the top branches of the tree, and the leaves look like trembling red flames. The whole tree is stretching upward, and suddenly many small birds fly up out of the branches.

A wind is rising; it stirs the leaves, moves the branches. A memory comes to me of a spring morning on the desert when the wind was no gentle stirring of air and branch and tree but was violent, diabolical. Dust devils whirled over the sand dunes; new nests, recently built by the birds in the warm weeks at winter's end, were blown down, the eggs shattered. Some eggs had hatched. The baby birds fell to earth, helpless, indifferently destroyed. I tried to rescue them, but it was hopeless. One downy little bird tossed its head, cheep-cheep, and died in my hand.

I hated nature that morning. She is too much like us, like me, suffers the same split personality—is kind, is brutal, falls into fits of sudden destructive temper, and as suddenly turns a radiant smile. Like me, she needs to be loved into redemption.

This morning I love nature. I love the old tree gallantly putting out green leaves and making a place for the birds to nest. On Thursday I sing your praises, sister mother. You are our roothold; you nurture us, and we must protect you. There are many planes of thought in Francis's Thursday morning canticle. In the Church, Thursday is the day that the priest's vocation is celebrated, especially in relation to the establishment of the celebration of the Holy Eucharist. The Church, as rooted in the earth and rising toward heaven, was certainly in the poet's mind. He was a deeply scriptural man. Indeed, the little green book tells me that on Thursday, the dominant idea for the Office is "love of God shown by devotion to the Holy Eucharist." On Thursday the Church prays in a particular way for its priests, who carry on the teaching of Christ and reenact his story: the Word leaping down from heaven, joining itself to our dust; the Word to be rooted in earth. On Thursday of Holy Week, the priest washes the feet of the poor. Our feet must walk on earth, even when pavements cover it. My mind can grasp wholeness—my mind, that God-gift so often suspect, so often rejected! But only with my mind can I *think*.

Be praised, my Lord, on Thursday, for on this ordinary day of the week the earth is bread and wine, and the Word comes down from heaven to enter the earth. Without the Word we would be like the little birds blown out of the nest, dying in the blasting, mindless wind. Without the bread and wine, the Word would lack substance. Thus I begin all over again each morning to put myself together, risking responsibility that demands mindfulness. My mind is also at stake on this earth, for it is here I am learning the art of seeing, an art learned here so slowly.

The art of seeing! I am constantly made anxious about using my mind. Intellectuality is feared among spiritual people just as much as, perhaps more than, it is feared among the general public. Spiritually minded people warn, "Beware of false intellectuality, intellectual pride." But there is the risk of false everything: false humility, pride in humility; false ignorance, mistaken for simplicity, and pride in false ignorance. The truth about intellectuality is that it is only the instrument given us to help us be mindful so that we may gain wisdom of heart. Mary the Mother of Christ is called the Mother of Wisdom, for Christ, her Son, is Wisdom.

Two roots: one descending, one ascending. The tree is bright now; the sunlight is glittering on every leaf, and the birds are flying in and out of it. A station wagon comes down the street, the first of the morning traffic, the early bird. The tires squeal as it halts, and a small boy jumps out, throws a newspaper over the curb. It lands on the wet ground. He jumps back in the car, and the woman at the wheel drives on.

Seeing him, I think of children—how they hate boredom, how they love to be stirred up. Children are delighted when you stir up their minds. Just yesterday I read a news story about missionaries in Lima, Peru, who had come to set up a medical dispensary but found they also had room for a library. One of the sisters decided to get books for the children who had no books with which to study. She said, "We didn't realize that we had struck a pastoral gold mine. We had often wondered how to reach the youth, and we had not been very successful. But when we opened this little library, we suddenly found ourselves surrounded by hundreds of boys and girls eager to learn."

Every day children came to be issued a book. They had to sit and read it right there in the reading room. No book could be taken home; the books were too few and too easily lost. More than a thousand young people came. The sister said: "We never were fully aware of this need. We have worked here for many years and only accidentally hit on this ministry. When we started this library we wondered if anyone would use it. Now we have more than a thousand users, and we meet more young people than ever before."

Talk about *lectio divina*—spiritual reading! Alleluia, be praised, my Lord, for our sister mother earth, who sustains and guides us and brings forth fruits of many kinds, with many-colored flowers and grass, especially reeds, from which we first learned to make parchment, and weeds, from which we learned to make ink. Be praised for trees and for books and newspapers that connect us up with the whole of our cosmos, and be praised for feet that walk in the dust and are washed by priests in the name of Christ.

Friday Morning at Lauds

It is very dark, and the rain is coming down hard, beating on the windows—surging waters trying to break in through the panes of glass.

I lie still, waiting for the idea of Friday to enter my consciousness—dawn and Friday. They come together for me now, and I realize today that Francis is rousing me so that I can be present at *The Dying*. He is directing my attention to the words of Lauds for Friday: they are about justice.

> Be praised, my Lord, for those who grant
>   pardon for love of you,
> And endure infirmity and tribulation.
> Blessed are they who maintain themselves in
>   peace,
> For from you, Most High, they shall have their
>   crown.
>
> *(Canticle of the Sun)*

Ever since Christ went up to Jerusalem to die on Friday, every Friday is Good Friday—in the contemplative way of Francis. I must get out of my warm bed on this dark, rain-swept dawn and take this journey. It is a personal journey, and Francis is teaching me that I am now deeply committed to a person-to-person relationship. My Lord is a person, a man, walking up the hill carrying a load, a heavy cross, going to his death today. Goodness and love have been condemned again today in our world of human justice, where the meting out of justice is measured by social and economic and political expediency. In the case of Christ, it was expedient that this man should die. In all times, human justice is meted out in a way that is not necessarily just, especially to the poor, who cannot afford to seek justice when unjustly treated, or to people of color, for example. It is *this* world Christ is talking about when he assures us that he has no part here. Our justice is not God's justice, the Bible says; yet we are bewildered when, in the Bible, Christ also warns that when he comes again he will condemn the world for *its* justice!

I'm not ready to go the journey Francis of Assisi takes me on. But anyway, with my lips I'll say the words. Today my contemporary is Julian, the fourteenth-century visionary who—"when she was thirty years old and a half"—was given "revelations of divine love." Christ spoke to her about justice, and she tells the experience. Christ spoke to her in fifteen "shewings" (showings), and it was during the ninth showing of himself to her that he told her he could never suffer too much for us.

The Ninth Revelation is the looking of the three heavens, and the infinite love of Christ desiring every day to suffer for us if he might, although it is not needful.

(*Revelations of Divine Love*)

Pain and suffering—why? The very words *pain* and *suffering* carry a great burden into my mind, and I think of Dostoyevsky in *The Brothers Karamazov*—his character Ivan compiling lists of the innocent sufferers, especially the children, the battered and abused children of whom there were so many in the nineteenth century, and of whom there are still so many in the twentieth century.

The Sanskrit word *siksanam*, like our word *suffering*, carries a weight of meanings: to educate, form, shape, elevate, punish. Suffering is at the heart of Christianity, as the exact test of love, the fire that purifies and trans-figures; yet it has more often been preached as a punish-ment for sin. I have always thought *that* preaching of suffering as punishment did more to negate the Chris-tian doctrine of love and to drain the spiritual energy generated by the Way of the Cross than any agnostic or atheistic arguments!

My teacher forces me to think more deeply about this terrible enigma. "Be praised, my Lord, for those who grant pardon for love of you." I repeat the words slowly.

Somehow pardon, forgiveness, is inherent in suffer-ing. Julian of Norwich heard Christ say these strange words: "Art thou well paid that I suffered for thee?" And instantly she responded: "Yes, good Lord, gra-mercy. Yes, good Lord, blessed mayst thou be." Then Jesus, her kind Lord, replied: "If thou art paid, I am paid: it is a joy, a bliss, and endless liking to me that ever suffered I passion for thee; and if I might suffer more, I would suffer more." And Julian saw that as often as he might die "so often he would, and love should never let him have rest till he had done it." She says, "I beheld with great diligence for to learn how often he would die if he might. And soothly the number passed mine understanding and my wits so far that my reason might not, nor could comprehend it. And when he had thus oft died, or should, yet he would set it at naught for love. . . . "

Julian, you lived many centuries before my time on this earth came, but when I step into this space called Lauds, I can take your hand. I would like to walk with your thoughts on this stormy morning, but I must stand and look from behind the glass, through this glass darkly, looking at this precious island, the earth, this pearl, as Shakespeare said unforgettably about his England. He was describing not just his own homeland,

but this world, our earth, the precious island floating in
the dark spaces of infinity and carrying our whole universe of time. Across the street the houses are dark, but
on the hills beyond, some lights are on. People there are
getting ready to go to work, to do the jobs that Friday
presents. I imagine what the lives of all the people on
these streets are like, and it seems to me that most of us
are the same in our longings, our deepest yearnings—
we would love to live in a world of peace and justice, to
love and be loved. From the depths, out of all the
biological urges, the attractions and repulsions, the sick
craziness manifested in our obsessions with pornography, sadism, drugs, death, torture, the longing to love
and be loved springs up. It can be polluted and mud-
died, but it is a living spring that keeps renewing itself,
and us.

Next door the girl who takes in many stray lovers
every day, every night, has been found beaten to death.
Across the street an out-of-work single mother has been
arrested for child abuse. When I moved away from the
desert and came to live here, near the sea, the world of
young sufferers was something I had to learn about.
Everyone says, "It's wonderful to be young." I see that
joy in physical activity, surfing, jogging, dancing, playing, making love, sexuality. But I also see the pitiful
frenzy, the fear of loneliness, desperate insecurity, fear
of getting old and funny-looking, and tragic confusions
of all kinds, especially about religion, cults, ethics,
morality, values. Most of all, in our America, there is
the nightmare threat that hangs over each generation
—to be a "loser."

Friday is for losers. Christ, the Lord of losers, is
carrying the day. Be praised, my Lord, for those who
endure infirmity and tribulation. The griefs of the
ages, the lovers with their arms around the griefs of the
ages, are my meditation, now, in this space of Lauds,

because it is Friday.

And my own griefs, which I remember too well and don't want to dig up again—but all this goes with me if I am to walk with Francis of Assisi on the way of the cross. All *things* must be brought with me on this path, this way of things, of *cosa*: I am bringing everything I have on this trip. Memory. Remember me, says Christ as he breaks the bread and gives a piece to everybody there. Remember me, says the King who has been murdered, to his son Hamlet, who goes mad with the memory of it all. Remember, man and woman, that you are dust and unto dust you shall return, says Ecclesiastes. Without the breath of God blown into our dust, we are but dust.

"Strengthening the memory of God within one's heart is a long and arduous process." Michael Casey's words—I have been reading him in *Cistercian Studies.* He goes on:

> The very act of memory is already an act of love, the desire to make present the absent Object of one's affections. . . . Memory is seen not simply as a faculty or skill for retrieving stored information; it is understood as a means for making contact with ultimate reality which although always present is habitually "forgotten" or ignored.

The religious person who lives in a convent or monastery is trained anew each day, each night, in the work of making contact with ultimate reality, through the prayers of the hours, the canonical office—strengthening the memory of God within the heart. But what of *me?* What of the man and the woman who are also longing to make "the very act of memory" their "act of love"; to strengthen the memory of God in their hearts?

My memory—the memory of an ordinary woman—is like a bird's nest, put together from bits of string, pieces of cotton batting from an old mattress, combings from somebody else's hair, sticks, straws from an unwieldy broom, dead twigs from an old rosebush full of thorns. In this nest are many small speckled eggs, some are broken; they never hatched. Others brought forth life that grew and developed, or died. I don't take death easily. I take death hard, the deaths of animals, birds, babies, children, sisters, brothers, a father that dies too young, an old mother that dies too old; friends and lovers. I take death hard. Somebody is breathing in the crib near the bed, a tiny person, making fascinating, lovable, strange noises of a baby breathing. Then the tiny person stops breathing. No sound will come ever again from the crib near the bed—the sound ceases forever.

Be praised, my Lord, for those who grant pardon for love of you. But how can I grant pardon when the one I must pardon is you, Lord? When Francis teaches me this Good Friday prayer, he is aware—the good teacher is always aware—that this ordinary woman, me, has a beginning to make when she is embarking on the immense task of granting pardon for love of Christ. She has to begin way back—she has to forgive God! She has to discover that Good Friday means rescue from death. On Good Friday, Christ, even he—still living through all that must be lived if one be truly mortal— reproached God: "My God, my God, why have you for- saken me?" He had to plumb the depths, and I, if I mean to walk this route, have to plumb those depths.

Thomas Hardy on his deathbed remembered lines from the *Rubaiyat* of Omar Khayyám, and spoke them to the God he did not and did believe in:

Oh, Thou, who man of baser Earth didst make,
And ev'n with Paradise devise the Snake:
    For all the Sin wherewith the Face of Man
Is blacken'd—Man's forgiveness give—and take!

Pondering this, I think about women being included in the word *man*. Women need to be mentioned as women, and especially in regard to forgiveness. Woman's forgiveness give—and take!

Caryll Houselander wrote that God hates death and that's why he went to all the bother of being born as a human, personal God, living our lives and dying our deaths—going through all the blood, sweat, and tears to rescue us from the finality of death. That was not the *end* for which we are created—not *The End*.

When Francis of Assisi was suffering the last months of his agony, he was visited by his doctor. Francis asked how much longer he had, but the doctor didn't want to tell him the truth. Francis said, "Don't think that I'm afraid of dying." He convinced the doctor, and the doctor said, "It will be over with you by the end of September or the beginning of October." Francis cried, "Welcome, brother death!" His companions Angelo and Leo were nearby. He said to them, "Sing me the song of death." He had composed the poem during his painfully long illness. With tears in their eyes they sang, and as they finished, Francis joined them, singing a new strophe: "Praised be you, my Lord, for our brother bodily death!"

Perhaps that would be very uplifting if it were then over, but he had ahead many dark, drawn-out months, of daily living of his dying. He had to discover how much compassion poor Brother Body needed during the long hours when a good plucky body, fighting death, struggles to go on breathing.

I think of all the well-wishers to the dying, who wish them most of all to get it over with, not to struggle to breathe—especially religious people! Religious people should be edifying, die peaceably with hands folded on their breasts and eyes raised to heaven—they set a bad example, struggling to breathe.

Poor Brother Body! Francis has been almost alone
among the saints who teach us to have compassion for
our bodies, as if they were little donkeys carrying Christ
up to Jerusalem to die. I think of John Howard Griffin.
In his last illness—suffering great pain from congestive
heart failure, osteomyelitis, one leg amputated and not
healing, diabetes—he was touched by the brave fight
the body put up. God had given him this body. He
looked with compassion on poor Brother Body, and
instead of futile ragings at the body for breaking down,
he watched with loving concern its struggle to go on
breathing, to recover energy. He was moved to grati-
tude and pity, as for some good little animal given him
to ride on up to Jerusalem. Do not whip this poor beast.

"Be praised, my Lord, for those who grant pardon
for love of you."

Everything must be granted pardon for love of
Christ. I, too, have to be granted pardon for love of
Christ. And I have to grant pardon for love of Christ; I
must think thoughts of love, not of resentment. If I am
to be granted pardon along with "everything" that
"must be granted pardon for love of Christ"—then?
Then I must grant pardon. I have to give up my bitterness, the hurts that are unpurged in the depths of consciousness. Memory must come up out of the
suffocating darkness, as Anne Lindbergh wrote after
the terrible knowledge came into her mind at last, from
the messengers who have to let you know, that her baby
was dead. These griefs sink down into the depths of our
souls and stay there, and we go down and stay there,
clasping them to our hearts, with our arms around the
griefs of the ages.

I feel as though I had been sleeping for years or
had lain in the lowest hold of a ship that, loaded
with heavy things, sailed through strange dis-
tances. Oh, to climb up on deck once more and

feel the winds and the birds, and to see how the great great nights come with their gleaming stars.
(Diaries and Letters, 1939-1944)

So this is prayer. This is Lauds—to climb up on deck once more.

Blessed are they who maintain themselves in
    peace,
For from you, Most High, they shall have their
    crown.

What are you saying, teacher? Yet another enigma. So here I am, lost in the darkness again, for *if* you are telling me to hold my peace and not mourn nor grieve, I cannot do it. Many deeply, sincerely religious people tell me not to mourn and say, "Carry on. Where is your faith? Why do you mourn like those who have no hope? Your child has not lost the end for which she was created. She is an immortal—for that she was born, not merely to be your pride and joy, but to be an immortal, to be God's pride and joy, and delight the Lord forever. So dry your tears."

Is that what you are saying, Francis of Assisi, when you teach me to pray at Lauds: "Blessed are they who maintain themselves in peace"? Keep still? Don't disturb the peace with your tears and lamentations?

The rain is still coming down hard, but the morning is getting lighter. A sad gray light is filtering through the curtain of rain; cars with their lights on are making loud swishing sounds as the tires ride through the water.

Christ did not maintain himself in peace—if peace means not to mourn or cry out. Christ cried out. Maybe the ones who scold about "lack of trust" are the ones who ought to be scolded. Most of the time they really want you to stop grieving because you're making everybody unhappy or at least uncomfortable. Christ made everybody uncomfortable, and that's what comes into

my mind—most comfortingly! He didn't leave anybody
"in peace." Just as he warns that his justice is not "the
world's" justice, so his idea of peace is not the world's
idea of peace—it doesn't mean unfeelingness. So Francis of Assisi, singing "Blessed are they who maintain
themselves in peace," isn't telling us not to grieve, not
to bother people. If I don't grieve and bother people,
they'll think death is just one of those things you have to
be routine about; it happens all the time, no big thing—
and then Christ's whole life, his life's work, is for nothing. On Good Friday Christ speaks about this to all who
go into a church and pay attention to the liturgy. He
says, "I looked for someone to weep with me, and there
was no one."

So I ask you, teacher, what do you mean by "Blessed
are they who maintain themselves in peace"? And I
hear your answer: "Keep loving God, hang in there,
don't let your suffering turn you into a cynic, keep the
faith, keep trusting in God's love, and bring *him* your
anger, your resentment, your unhealing wound; bring
him your hurt. That's what it means. Blessed are they
who maintain themselves in peace means *not* to keep a
stiff upper lip, but to hang on, keep loving and trusting,
and be truthful. Be truthful with God; bring everything
out and give it to him."

I don't have to be a stoic or a hypocrite. All I have to
do is live through each of these days, whatever each day
brings—say *yes.* The suffering never disappears, but
the conflict disappears. Francis makes you mindful; he
makes prayer a work of thought as well as of spirituality.
It's possible that a work of thought is necessary in
prayer, and that's why the prayer of *cosa* makes me
bring everything to my relationship with God. It ends
up with my breaking out of my own grief and perhaps
achieving that union with all who grieve, which is the
sign that God is present.

Francis was in pain when he wrote these Praises. It was spring, 1225, and he went to San Damiano to visit Saint Clare. But soon after he arrived he collapsed, and they had to put him in a cell and take care of him. During those days, sick unto death, he wrote his greatest poems. The *Canticle of Praises* is today recognized as the most beautiful poem-series in the Italian language, and indeed, even in translation into many languages. It was among the first poems written in the vernacular, the language of the common people, because Francis was the teacher for ordinary people (as well as for religious in convents and monasteries). Francis saw the whole world as a novitiate, and centuries later, the twentieth-century English mystic Caryll Houselander took her stand in his space, writing:

> The world, the ordinary world of everyday, has always been and is now, the best school of suffering. There is no novitiate so searching, none other where God alone is novice-master, and where Christ is learned so truly.

She lived in the time shortly before Vatican II, when teachers of prayer encouraged the seeker to get away from "the world"—to find some place far from worldly things in order to be a contemplative. There are many such teachers, even now, who seem to teach prayer as an exit from "the world."

Caryll Houselander tried to explain the distinctions that must be perceived by those who seek prayer:

> By "the world" I do not mean worldliness. I am not using the words now with the meaning that Christ gave them when He spoke of the world which hated Him and in which He had no part. By that Christ meant worldliness, the harshness of the Pharisees of His time and of all time, the cunning of the hypocrites, the complacency and selfishness

of the rich both then and now. . . . By "the
world" as I use the expression here, I mean the
environment in which the majority of us now live.
(The Comforting of Christ)

What Francis of Assisi teaches me this Friday morning is that no truthful prayer is an "escape" from the
world. The pollution, the hard rain, the fallout from
the bombs fall on the contemplative sitting cross-legged
on a mountaintop, on the mystic walking through the
woods, on the streets and the freeways—on rich and
poor and middle class, on all the most elaborately constructed underground bomb shelters, too.

> Be praised, my Lord, for those who grant
>   pardon for love of you,
> And endure infirmity and tribulation.
> Blessed are they who maintain themselves in
>   peace,
> For from you, Most High, they shall have their
>   crown.

I am taking this journey with you on Friday, today; I
go forth weeping to sow whatever seed is *me*, and I trust
I will return carrying my sheaves, singing. It is good to
stand in any small space and pray Lauds, because praise
is humble and Christ will hear it from my street as much
as from the mountaintop, the forest, from a church, a
synagogue, or a tent. Love is humble, and Christ will be
anywhere.

There's a story from the Jewish *Talmud* about the son
of a king who abandoned his inheritance and went away,
like the prodigal son. The son had a bad time, and when
his father, the king, heard reports of his son's troubles,
he sent a messenger to ask him to come back. The son
replied, in guilt and shame, "I cannot." Then his father
sent a second messenger with a message: "Come back as
far as you can, and I will come to meet you there."

We pray, each of us, in our own way. Prayer is very personal and uniquely our own, yet there is a universal motivation, a universal journey that is the same for all of us, and I think this *Talmud* story sums it up—to come back as far as we can.

The window, streaming with water, makes the road outside appear like an eroded shoreline. Loren Eiseley tells a story: Early one morning he was walking by the sea. Dozens of starfish had been washed up by the tides and now could never get back—their spores were filled with sand. When the sun rose they would shrink and die. "The sea-beach and its endless war are soul-less," he wrote, depressed. He noticed someone walking in that same dawn, on the same beach, who was picking up one starfish, then another, and spinning them far out to sea. Eiseley drew close to him. The stranger explained, "Some may live—if the offshore pull is strong enough. The stars throw well—one can help them." He, too, began picking up starfish and throwing them back into the sea.

It's light now, and I must step out of this space called Lauds. I must step back into time—maybe I'll throw a starfish back into the sea.

Good Friday is not the end but the beginning. After Friday comes Saturday—the Church calls the Saturday before the Sunday of the Resurrection, Holy Saturday. On that day all is in darkness and the time of *nada* opens the abyss, the dark night of the soul.

Saturday Morning at Lauds

The week is wound up like a clock spring on my planet Earth, planet of time and timekeepers. The seventh day has begun, the seventh day since last Sunday, when I got up early in the morning to praise my God who makes all things, my Lord the maker.

> God saw all he had made, and indeed it was very good. Evening came and morning came: the sixth day.
> Thus heaven and earth were completed with all their array. On the seventh day God completed the work he had been doing. He rested on the seventh day after all the work he had been doing. God blessed the seventh day and made it holy, because on that day he had rested after all his work of creating.
>
> (Gen. 1:31; 2:1-3)

I am genesis-connected. Saturday is the end of my workweek, and it is also the day when Francis of Assisi calls me into the space where all is dark; I have arrived at *nada*—the dawn after the crucifixion of Christ on Friday.

Lauds. Praises must be sung in a loud voice, says my teacher, as I awaken to this spiritual darkness, the true dark night of the soul.

> Be praised, my Lord, for our brother the death
>   of the body,
> Which no one among the living can escape.
> Unhappy they who will die in mortal sin.

Blessed those who shall be found in your most
    holy pleasure,
For the second death shall do no harm to them.

(Canticle of the Sun)

I do not say the prayer in the exact words of the little green book. Instead of "unhappy they who will die in mortal sin," my prayer comes out: "Sad they who die still hating; they die in mortal sin"—because the opposite of love is hate. "Happy they who have clung steadfast to love of you," my own mind continues; "they shall be awakened in your holy pleasure."

Every Friday the God of Love dies. I think again of the words of Christ to Julian: "If thou art paid, I am paid: it is a joy, a bliss, and endless liking to me that ever suffered I passion for thee; and if I might suffer more, I would suffer more." Julian understood. She saw that as often as Christ might die, "so often he would, and love should never let him have rest till he had done it."

But at that instant in time when life ebbs away, the void enters into our souls. The sun goes out, the dark is suffocating, airless, lightless. Long before we die, we are given to know the experience of the void, the dark night of the soul, whenever a living creature dies.

When his wife died, C. S. Lewis wrote:

It is hard to have patience with people who say "There is no death" or "Death doesn't matter." There is death. And whatever is matters. And whatever happens has consequences, and it and they are irrevocable and irreversible. You might as well say that birth doesn't matter.

(A Grief Observed)

When my sister was dying, on her last night, though hundreds of miles away, I heard her voice weaving through the torpor of sleep, talking to me—a haunting, sad song: "I am sick, darling, awfully sick." It was strange, that sad melody singing in my ear, in my heart, and I could not wake myself up. I had a terrible pain in my stomach, and all I could do was respond in the drowsiness of that night, "Give me your stomachache, love. Lord, let me have the stomachache for my sister." This pathetic conversation went on through the night, hour after hour. Then very suddenly the sad song ceased. Nothingness. The invisible thread between us was broken.

Every person experiences a time of *nada*, when there is no need striving to empty yourself; the void pours in, and emptiness and darkness seem to overcome the light of hope, trust, steadfast love. I have only one candle in this darkness, the "Word" from the Gospel of St. John: "The Light shone in the darkness, and the darkness was not able to overcome it." (This is not a quote. The "Word" from the Gospel of St. John is in my memory this way, and I think and pray in my own words.)

My understanding of Saint Teresa of Avila's great prayer of *nada* is also part of my inner vocabulary, and I think of her words, not as praising *nada*, but as praising the trust, the faith, that the dark is not able to put out the Light, cannot master it, will not overcome.

She did not say that *nada* was the goal. What she said was, "Don't let it terrify you; it is only a space, a dark stretch we have to make our way through, like birds flying beyond their wing-capacity, letting the immortal current carry them across the void."

Nada te turba
nada te espante
todo se pasa
Dios no se mude
la paciencia
todo lo alcanza
Quien a Dios tiene
Nada le falta

Solo Dios basta!

(Saint Teresa's Bookmark)

The Spanish words resonate in my heart, but when I ponder them in my head, they speak to me in an English translation all my own:

Let nothing unnerve you, let nothing frighten
 you.
You will pass over—for all this is passing.
God alone remains. Just be patient;
patience attains *All*.
When you have God, nothing will be lacking.
God is sufficient. God is Everything.

On the nightstand there is a holy card. It is for the Jewish convert mystic Edith Stein—Sister Teresa Benedicta of the Cross. She died in Auschwitz.

O my God
fill my soul with holy joy
courage and strength
to serve you.
Enkindle your love in me
and then walk with me
along the next stretch
of ROAD before me.
I do not see very far ahead.
But when I have arrived where
the horizon now closes down,
a new prospect
will open before me
and I shall meet it with peace.

(Carmel of Des Plaines)

Saturday, the day of *nada*, the dark space that must be lived through, the dark void that we trust ourselves to, trusting the current to carry us across: Saturday I am down but must go up.

As I wake each morning to say Lauds with Francis, the prayers of the ages are in this space; the darkness is dark but not empty. Twenty centuries of Lauds, and now my century joining them, rise skyward with Jesus. But right now it is Saturday, the light is invisible, the thread is broken. On Holy Saturday before Easter, the altar is stripped, the candles are put out, the church is dark.

The ultimate trust must be in this moment in time when my teacher wakes me to step into the void and praise the Lord for the death of my body!

John of the Cross wrote that only in this void, this night, is the moment of trust valid. Everything is taken from me. My memory brings sadness and affliction, bitterness and anguish. My soul is deprived of the spiritual blessings that comfort me in the midst of nature, especially walking across the desert early in the morning with my dog and watching the first rays of sun light up the vastness of sky and the planes, curves—the wonderfully made earth. In the darkness of holy Saturday the tide overwhelms me, and I understand John of the Cross, especially his words:

It seems God is against the person and the person is against God. Both the sense and the spirit, as though under an immense and dark load, undergo such agony and pain that the soul would consider death a relief.

(The Collected Works)

Juan de la Cruz, Saint John of the Cross, you bring up even that Old Testament mourner Job. To me the most interesting thing about Job is not his sufferings, for I know all about them, and so does every man, woman, and child, all who live life through in this world. The most interesting thing about Job is his bad temper, his spiritedness, his shoutings and his despairs, too, because he would not let the void submerge and silence him; he would not let go. He hung on to all of his created life, his wife and children who had died, his boils, his stomachaches, his laborious sowing and reaping. He carried his world of time, like the mythical Greek Atlas, forced to support on his head and with his hands the pillars that held up the heavens. But Job carried earth itself, and went into the dark night, not letting go, carrying it across the emptiness, trusting in the divine current that would bring him and his whole load to the safe shore.

In my mind these two stories come together, Job and Atlas. For in some mysterious way, Job, by bearing the burden of his world, was thereby holding up heaven! That is what I think the Dominican theologian Schillebeeckx means when he says that Christ is the Sacrament of the Meeting with God, and that to be a Christian to the *limit* of your being is to bring your world wholly to this Meeting.

In the liturgy of the Mass, God gives me his body and blood, and I think that my response is to bring him my body and blood—my Eucharist, which is the earth. This is the meeting toward which I go, getting up each morning to begin again, simply trusting, with no light except the dim candlelight of faith to guide me. The earth is my Eucharist. Each of us has this eucharistic task to bring to this meeting—may it be a meeting that does not go wrong.

Julian of Norwich writes:

There was a treasure in the earth which the Lord loved. . . . I saw in the Lord that he hath within himself endless life, all manner of goodness, save that treasure that was in the earth. And also that treasure was grounded in the Lord in marvellous deepness of endless love, but it was not all to his

worship till the Servant had thus nobly prepared it,
and brought it before him.
                              (*Revelations of Divine Love*)

There is "a treasure in the earth which the Lord
loves," and I am one of the carriers. Everyone who lives
is given that option: to be a carrier of this treasure in the
earth that the Lord loves. That is why our egos are
essential: There is only one of *me*; there will never be a
fingerprint like mine again. Each of us has a unique
portion of this earth to live on and in and through. To
bring to God what we alone have lived through, our
world, is to bring what no other person can bring.

There was a priest in France who became famous as
one of the "worker priests." He was born in 1914 and
died young, in 1954. His name was Henri Perrin. He
had a vision in which he saw that the whole world was
consecrated, sacred:

> The whole universe is sacred from the fact that it
> finds its unity in Christ. . . . Sometimes I get the
> impression that the world we live in, the world as
> depicted in novels and movies and in the newspa-
> pers, seems to us purely and simply the kingdom of
> evil not yet divinized. Whereas a vision of genuine
> faith seems to me to demand that we view the
> world not only as wrestling with God but also as
> already making its way slowly toward Him,
> through the Incarnation.
>   (*Priest and Worker*)

This is the way Francis of Assisi perceived the world,
and the way he teaches those who go according to his
instructions, learning his way of prayer. At Lauds I
begin all over again, starting from my own little acre
where I live, starting from my own self, and I try to
construct "an *opus.*"

Teilhard de Chardin says we do not know under what guise our natural selves will pass over into the divine vision, but we cannot doubt that, with God's help, it is here below that we give ourselves the eye and the heart.

The eye and the heart: The eye that sees is another way of saying "mindfulness"; the heart that feels is another way of saying "compassion." Teresa of Avila taught this as the motivation for all prayer:

> The reason for prayer, my daughters, the purpose of the spiritual marriage, is the birth of good works always, good works. . . . Compassion is born in one who enters the spiritual marriage and is likewise the only way to achieve this union with God.
>
> (*The Collected Works*)

Compassion for all that lives, compassion for our sister mother earth; compassion for the air, and for the waters: the rivers, the lakes with dead fish, the seas with the dead birds from the oil spills. God gave us dominion. We are only beginning to understand that dominion means compassion, a teaching that was set aside when the stories were told about Francis of Assisi. They sentimentalize him.

"WE ARE THE BEES OF THE INVISIBLE," the poet Rilke wrote. For me, the words are always as the poet heard them; he heard them in uppercase, and in his tremendous Ninth Elegy, his voice rings out:

> Earth, isn't this what you want: an invisible re-arising in us?

That is the task of transformation as the poet Blake saw, too: to bring forth honey from the rock.

When the Lord delivers us from bondage it will seem like a dream, and our mouths will be filled with laughter; on our lips there will be songs.

One morning I saw the black comedian Richard
Pryor on television, being interviewed after his near-
dying from fire. It was fire of his own making, and the
interviewer asked if it was a suicide try. The comedian
admitted it was, and the interviewer quickly interrupted
with ". . . which failed." But Pryor just as quickly
replied, ". . . which succeeded—I killed the old man."
He went on to tell the sudden, shocking experience of
joy for the first time in a miserable life. His mother,
though a good mother, had been a prostitute; he grew
up on the streets, and drugs had come early in childhood. When he nearly burned himself up alive, something happened—a different kind of light struck him:
not the destructive light of the fire that was burning his
clothes, his hair, his skin, but the kind of fire that struck
Saul like a blinding light on the road to Damascus. And
suddenly life was no longer evil, a living hell; life was
good! Life was Good! He experienced the thing that
can only be described as mystical joy. The interviewer
asked: "How does such an experience feel?" Richard
Pryor looked bewildered and then said in a wondering
voice, "Bad! Because I never experienced joy. I wasn't
used to that kind of feeling."

Listening, I tried to copy his words down as best I
could, for I wanted to keep them and think about them.
He said that just thinking that life is good was something he was not used to—such a thought confused him.
"I didn't know how to react to joy. I didn't know how to
react to goodness. I was used to reacting to badness."

He was used to being unhappy and hating life and
thinking life was hell. "I didn't know how to react to
heaven, to goodness, to joy—it confused me."

We are so used to evil, we take corruption, pornography, torture, rape, murder, assassination, even the idea
that it's all right to live underground in an atomic shelter, a bomb shelter, while outside the world is writhing,

destroyed—we take it all in stride! So when goodness breaks in, it's hard to grasp. We are dazed, confused. When the Lord delivers us from bondage, it seems like a dream.

Saint John of the Cross says that a soul must pass through two kinds of night. In his beautiful poem *The Dark Night* he describes the soul going forth into the darkness, on fire with love for God, pulled by *that* magnet:

> One dark night,
> Fired with love's urgent longings
> —Ah, the sheer grace!—
> I went out unseen,
> My house being now all stilled.
>
> (*The Collected Works*)

He explains that the words "my house being now all stilled" mean that through grace the senses are quieted, and although "one is not freed from the sufferings and anguish of appetites until they are tempered," yet one is able, by sheer grace of God, to go forth. The road is faith.

Francis of Assisi draws me along the same road, and I trust myself, timidly, to take that walk in the darkness, not because I am quieted and my senses are at last tempered, but because his teaching of compassion for all that lives has given me a job to do, something I must carry through this night, for which I am responsible, and which I alone can do.

In the dark I cannot see the earth, but I feel it under my feet. This earth is also my body, this part on which I walk every day, every night. Only through me will it be immortalized. My dog sees much better in the dark than I do, even as it is written in the Old Testament: The dog saw that an angel was with Tobias, his human master, when they set forth on their journey. But

Tobias didn't. Yet my dog, despite all his knowing and courage, presses his head against my hip, for he senses I am timid and groping my way in the dark. This creature is my charge, part of the "dominion" God gave humans. Only through me may he be immortalized.

All creation yearns for this transfiguration, the immortal state when all our potentials are realized. So said Paul the Apostle. All creation groans for salvation, and what is salvation but the perfection of love?

God tells me in scripture that his thoughts are not my thoughts, that he thinks thoughts of love, not of destruction. But *me*? Here am I this Saturday at dawn, in the total dark of Holy Saturday after Good Friday, still striving to make altitude, to make this skyward climb, with prayer as my lift-off energy. Why?

Not for the excitement or the sensationalism of a different kind of trip. Not to go to heaven and play a gold harp and float around in a white robe. Not even to foresee my Nothingness absorbed in God's All, as the rapture of the beatific vision is explained to me. Nor even to be forgiven, to be shown mercy—not in the sense most religious writers expound.

To love and be loved, said Saint Thérèse of Lisieux— even though I don't know what that really is; that's *it*, that's my *why*! The poet Keats wrote that this world is the vale of soul-making, but in heaven where there is true philosophy, even the nightingale sings in philosophic tones. He did not mean by philosophy what the scholars mean; he meant mindfulness, being *awake* in eye and heart. The disciples of Buddha asked him if he was God. He said no. Then they asked who he was. He said: "I am *Awake*." The word *Buddha* means *awake*. The disciples of Christ asked him if he was God. He did not say no, but he answered in such a way that he spared them the second question. That is, his answer was to tell them who he was: "I am the *Resurrection*." To be *Awake* is essential, and it is profoundly part of the *Resurrection*.

My teacher, who follows the words of Christ, the Christ of the Gospels and of the Church, to an austere degree, teaches that the Resurrection includes the body. God, who became a man, who became flesh in the act henceforth known as the incarnation, gives me a body destined for immortality! This is the ultimate Christian difference. The Resurrection includes my body, not just my soul.

My teacher won't let me off on any emotional nature-love binges. He takes me on no sentimental journey. What Francis of Assisi does try to develop in me is praise of all that is God's making, praise of beauty and praise of ugliness—loving the play of the fountain, the graceful leap of a beautiful wolf, the ringing sound of a lark rising into the sky. And loving the humping three-legged cat, the legless old man, the shrunken-breasted old woman, the brain-damaged child, kissing the lepers, lowly and repulsive.

"In each soul," writes Teilhard de Chardin, "God loves and partly saves the whole world which that soul sums up in an incommunicable and particular way."

To take the way of contemplation with Francis of Assisi, I have to change old habits. Time! Suddenly time is much more serious, much less boring, too; indeed time is exciting, but oh so demanding: Noiseless, inaudible bells wake me up to pray the canonical hours. Then there is the paradox of time, that it is exciting because it is the door that opens into timelessness. Time must have a stop. I use time to get out of time, to get into timeless space. Another thing Francis of Assisi makes me realize is that I can't be vague or abstract about God. Just as God takes me in all my reality, a real person, so I have to learn that my God is no vague divinity, but a Person; God is *Someone*.

All teachers of prayer exalt purification, especially

through annihilation of the ego. But the way of *cosa*, unlike the way of *nada*, is not detachment nor self-perfection; it is the way of the eye and the heart: compassion and responsibility (God gave us dominion; once again the same phrase echoes throughout).

Francis of Assisi teaches a radical way of contemplative prayer that culminates on Saturday, connects my week's ordinary Saturday to Holy Saturday—in a different mindfulness about death. Mindfulness, because when I step off this shore and trust myself to the outward-bound current on that dark sea, my radical God expects me to be able to stay afloat though carrying my whole world; *everything*, not only all God's makings being returned to God, but all my makings, and everything I ever read—the books, the paintings and the movies, the ballets, the sonatas and the concertos, and all the songs.

In some churches an Office of Tenebrae is celebrated during the time before Easter—the word *tenebrae* means darkness. During this Office all the lights are gradually put out, until only one candle is left flickering. This flickering candle is hidden behind the altar where no one can catch even a glimmer of its light. The church is in total darkness. The dark is thick and heavy, frightening; *nada*. But the light of the hidden candle is there. You can't see it, but it's there, the *cosa*, the thing is there—a lit candle invisible behind the altar. It is like the spiderweb that just brushes my arms as I walk the dark of this predawn on Saturday. The silver thread is there, but I can't see it. And as I go on, I no longer feel the spiderweb, only the darkness waiting for the light, when earth-time opens and I enter cosmic time.

Come Back as Far as You Can

Some mornings it is too hard. I can't rise at dawn to sing the praises of Lauds. All night someone I love has been very sick, and just when the need for prayer is most urgent, I cannot pray; there is only weariness and torpor.

But I know the time. There is some deep thing going on inside me just because I know this is the hour of Lauds; *that* is also prayer. "Even in our dreams," says Eknath Easwaran, "we can learn to dispel fear and anger." The simple nod of recognition is a way of being present just as I am. Yet I am not "just as I am" anymore. I *know* about Lauds. My life is enhanced by that knowing. The parable of the talents comes into my mind. That tale of the landowner who has to go away and gives his workers talents (money) has always bothered me. The two who invest their talents are praised when the landowner returns home, but he throws the third man out, because that man buried his money in the earth instead of investing it for a good return! To me this seems unjust. The poor man was probably a timid person who knew he was a loser, and feared to invest his talent because it was "just his luck" he would lose it all.

On this dreary Saturday before dawn, at this time of Lauds, a new thought comes: "Something is expected of me." God expects a return, indeed an enhanced return. I owe him a life. The common saying is that everyone owes God a death, but the directing force of the prayer of *cosa* changes that. We all owe God a life.

References

Introduction

Frederick Buechner, *The Sacred Journey* (New York: Harper & Row, 1982), p. 6.

Office of the Paters (Chicago: Franciscan Herald Press, 1949).

J. D. Salinger, *Franny and Zooey* (New York: Bantam Books, 1964), p. 176; pp. 36, 37.

The Cloud of Unknowing (London: John M. Watkins, 1950).

Maurice Samuel, *The World of Sholom Aleichem* (New York: Alfred A. Knopf, 1943), pp. 11, 12.

Sunday Morning at Lauds

Office of the Paters, p. 27.

Thomas Merton, *Emblems of a Season of Fury* (New York: New Directions, 1963), pp. 61-66.

Office of the Paters, pp. 57, 58.

The Collected Works of St. John of the Cross, trans. Kieran Kavanaugh, OCD, and Otilio Rodriguez, OCD (Washington, D.C.: ICS Publications, 1973), p. 79.

Thomas Merton, *The Last of the Fathers* (New York: Harcourt, Brace, 1954), p. 11.

Rainer Maria Rilke, *Duino Elegies* (New York: Norton, 1939), p. 73.

Pierre Teilhard de Chardin, *The Divine Milieu* (New York: Harper & Bros., 1960).

Lawrence Cunningham (text) and Dennis Stock (photos), *Saint Francis of Assisi* (San Francisco: Harper & Row, 1981), p. 60.

Thomas Merton, *Zen and the Birds of Appetite* (New York: New Directions, 1968), pp. 99-103.

William McNamara, *Earthy Mysticism* (New York: Crossroad, 1983), p. 12.

Monday Morning at Lauds

Office of the Paters, p. 33.
Rafael Alberti, *The Lost Grove* (Berkeley: University of California Press, 1964).
Jacques Maritain, *Existence and the Existent* (New York: Image Books, 1956), p. 80.
Thomas Merton, *The Sign of Jonas* (New York: Image Books, 1956), p. 51.
Thomas Merton, *The Sign of Jonas* (New York: Image Books, 1956), p. 124.
Swami Vivekananda, *Bhakti-Yoga, The Yoga of Love and Devotion* (Calcutta, India: Advaita Ashrama, 1978), p. 71.

Tuesday Morning at Lauds

Office of the Paters, p. 40.
Gerard Manley Hopkins, *Poems* (New York: Oxford University Press, 1948), p. 99.
Thomas Merton, *Emblems of a Season of Fury*, p. 67.
Office of the Paters, p. 69.
Lewis Thomas, *The Youngest Science, Notes of a Medicine-Watcher* (New York: Viking, 1983), pp. 89-90.
Sir Bernard Lovell, *In the Center of the Immensities* (New York: Harper & Row, 1978).
Morris Berman, *The Reenchantment of the World* (Cornell University Press, 1981).
James W. Kunetka, *Oppenheimer, The Years of Risk* (New Jersey: Prentice-Hall, 1982), pp. 65-75.
Alfred Delp, S.J., *The Prison Meditations* (New York: Macmillan, 1963).
The Collected Works of St. John of the Cross, p. 89.

Wednesday Morning at Lauds

Office of the Paters, p. 46.

George Fox, *Journal* (New York: Dutton, 1969), p. 9.

Eknath Easwaran in a personal conversation with the author. Eknath Easwaran established the Blue Mountain Center for Meditation, Berkeley, California, in 1960.

Dom Justin McCann, *St. Benedict* (New York: Sheed & Ward, 1957), p. 205.

G. K. Chesterton, *St. Francis of Assisi* (New York: Image Books, 1957), p. 154.

André Billy, *Max Jacob* (Paris: Editions Pierre Seghers, 1947).

Cunningham and Stock, *Saint Francis of Assisi.*

Fyodor Dostoyevsky, *The Brothers Karamazov* (New York: Halcyon House, 1940).

The Little Flowers & the Life of St. Francis with the Mirror of Perfection (London: J. M. Dent & Sons, 1910); *Everyman's Library* (New York: E. P. Dutton, 1912).

Bhakti-Yoga, The Yoga of Love and Devotion, p. 109.

Thursday Morning at Lauds

Office of the Paters, p. 52.

Friday Morning at Lauds

Office of the Paters, p. 59.

Julian of Norwich, *Revelations of Divine Love* (London: Burns Oates, 1952), p. 40.

Michael Casey, "Mindfulness of God in the Monastic Tradition," *Cistercian Studies* 17 (1982): 111-126.

Florence Emily Hardy, *The Later Years of Thomas Hardy, 1892-1928* (New York: Macmillan, 1930), p. 266.

Anne Lindbergh, *Diaries and Letters, 1939-1944* (New York: Harcourt, Brace, Jovanovich, 1980).

Caryll Houselander, *The Comforting of Christ* (New York: Sheed & Ward, 1947), p. 104.

Saturday Morning at Lauds

Office of the Paters, p. 66.

C. S. Lewis, *A Grief Observed* (New York: Seabury, 1961), p. 16.

The Collected Works of St. Teresa of Avila, trans. Kieran Kavanaugh, OCD, and Otilio Rodriguez, OCD, vol. 1 (Washington, D.C.: ICS Publications, 1976).

For a more literal translation of "the words of Teresa's bookmark":

> Let nothing disturb you
> Let nothing frighten you
> All things are passing.
> God never changes.
> Patience obtains all things
> Whoever has God wants nothing.
> God alone suffices.

I have taken this from an article by Bishop Eugene A. Marino, SSJ, Auxiliary Bishop of Washington, D.C., "A Homily: Mass in Honor of Saint Teresa of Avila," in *Spiritual Life* (Fall 1982).

The bookmark from which my Spanish quotation comes was sent to me from Spain. It is very old, and the print that tells the source is illegible.

Holy card with Edith Stein's prayer has after it: Sr. Teresa Benedicta of the Cross (her name as a religious), and comes from Carmel of Des Plaines.

The Collected Works of St. John of the Cross, p. 77.

Revelations of Divine Love, p. 98.

Henri Perrin, *Priest and Worker* (Chicago: Henry Regnery Co., 1966), p. 144.

The Collected Works of St. Teresa of Avila, vol. 1.

Duino Elegies, p. 128.

The Collected Works of St. John of the Cross, p. 73.

The Divine Milieu, p. 29.